MODELLING
BRITISH AIRCRAFT
OF WORLD WAR II

MODELLING
BRITISH AIRCRAFT
OF WORLD WAR II

JEFF HERNE

THE CROWOOD PRESS

First published in 2020 by
The Crowood Press Ltd
Ramsbury, Marlborough
Wiltshire SN8 2HR

enquiries@crowood.com

www.crowood.com

British Library Cataloguing-in-Publication Data
A catalogue record for this book is available from the British Library.

ISBN 978 1 78500 781 1

Designed and typeset by Guy Croton Publishing Services,
West Malling, Kent

Printed and bound in India by Replika Press Pvt Ltd

Contents

Dedication and Acknowledgements

This book is dedicated to my loving wife Laura and daughter Katelyn, who not only tolerated my countless hours in the shop, but countless hours at the computer putting thoughts and details into words. I am a lucky man to have such wonderful ladies in my life.

Special thanks must be extended to the following people, without whose assistance this work would not have been possible.

Dave Raatz – when I wanted to sleep, he told me to write.

David Holmes – who took the ramblings of a Yank and turned them into respectable English.

Shannon O'Neill, Wayne Dippold, Ronnie MacDonald, Vic Scheuerman, Seb Sherburn, Jeff Barrette, Dave Gayton and Chris Henry at the EAA Museum in Oshkosh, for allowing me access to their photo collections and their aircraft. What better way to research a Mossie than from the cockpit?

Photos credited to Australian War Memorial, US National Archives, Smithsonian National Air and Space Museum, United States Air Force, Canadian National Archives, Archives New Zealand, Fleet Air Arm Museum, Imperial War Museum and British Ministry of Defence are in the public domain or carry an Open Government Licence (OGL v.1). Individual credits are given where known. All other photos are from the author's collection.

Introduction

HURRICANE. SPITFIRE. MOSQUITO. SWORDFISH. LANCASTER ...

These are some of the most legendary aircraft to emerge from World War II. Since their introduction in the 1930s and 1940s, models have been made of them, first in wood, then plastic, and today there are hundreds of kits of these aircraft available to the hobbyist in a huge array of scales and variants. It is safe to say that millions of models of these aircraft have been built over the years by both expert and novice modellers alike.

But what defines an expert modeller from a novice? Many will assume that it is the experience of the builder or the tools and techniques that define what the ultimate end result will be – a model worthy of a place in a museum, or a fair representation of an aircraft in miniature form for your bookshelf.

With the explosive growth of the Internet and social media, scale modelling became a worldwide, interconnected hobby and suddenly modellers were communicating with other like-minded builders all over the planet, discussing kits and techniques and sharing the history we attempt to convey through our models. Despite this tremendous resource of information, after a few minutes online one immediately notices that not everyone is ahead of the curve, qualitatively speaking. As modellers, we develop techniques over time, through trial and error, and when we find something that works tend to become reluctant to change our ways. Sometimes, that can be a hindrance.

As a professional modeller, I am always searching for ways to improve my efficiency, improve my product and minimize the frustrations and hurdles we have all had to overcome in our beloved pastime. At the same time, I have learnt to balance the hobby and the job – despite the fact that both are the exact same thing. Despite four decades in this hobby, I am still learning new techniques and methods, and not necessarily from the 'expert' modeller, but from someone new to the hobby who saw a problem and developed a common-sense technique that was superior to mine.

While I cannot promise you that this volume will make you an expert, I can promise you that if you have ever looked upon others' work and wished you could achieve similar results, then our goal is to reduce your learning curve, minimize trial and error and help you to achieve those same results.

Jeff Herne
Ixonia, Wisconsin, USA

Chapter One

Preparation

We shall start off under the impression that this is not only your first serious model kit as an adult – but it is the first model you have ever attempted. If you are an experienced modeller this could be a tad repetitive, but you never know what little bits of information you may pick up along the way. If you're not an expert, start out with the understanding that this is not a race; rather, it is a journey that requires time and patience to master, and once you feel you've mastered it, another challenge will come along to motivate your creativity.

Regardless of your skill level or experience, the journey you are about to set upon is not about simply building a miniature version of your favourite aircraft – it's far more than that. You are, in essence, creating art. Your model will be a reflection of the effort and passion you put into it. Only you can decide to what level you take your work in terms of accuracy and detail. In order to accomplish these goals, you must be prepared with some basic knowledge. There are countless things to consider when building a model. The complexity of the kit, the tools and resources at your disposal to physically construct the kit, and even your attitude going into the project, all contribute to the end result.

Selecting a kit to build is not a random act. For some, it's the most difficult part of the process. Perhaps it's the look of the model, perhaps you have a historical connection to the original aircraft or pilot. Whatever the reason, the key to your initial success is choosing a model you are capable of building and completing within a reasonable amount of time. What this means, simply, is to start out with a kit that you can actually finish

SPITFIRE SCALE DIMENSIONS

How big is big? Choose your scales wisely, especially if space is at a premium:

- the wingspan of a 1/72 scale Spitfire is 6in (152mm)
- the wingspan of a 1/48 scale Spitfire is 9.25in (235mm)
- the wingspan of a 1/32 scale Spitfire is 15in (380mm) (but a 1/32 scale Lancaster has a wingspan of 38.25in [972mm]!).

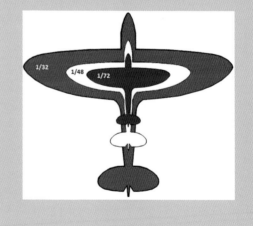

without being overwhelmed by its complexity or physical size. A single-seat fighter such as a Spitfire or Hurricane will allow you to gain experience and confidence, while also developing construction techniques without being intimidated by the overall scope of the project.

Fig. 1.1 Choose a scale based on your available space, budget and eyesight.

The scale of the kit is also important. A 1/72 Spitfire is an evening's worth of building, whereas 1/48 and 1/32 scale kits will require proportional amounts of time to complete, as the level of detail inherently increases with the physical size of the model. The construction averages will vary based on the modeller's skills and experience, but the average modeller should invest fifteen to twenty hours of time on a 1/72 scale Spitfire, twenty-five to thirty hours of time on a 1/48 scale Spitfire, and forty hours or more on a 1/32 scale kit, based on a typical, out of the box build. A super-detailed 1/32 scale model is likely to require several hundred hours of work if done properly.

There are several factors to consider when selecting a scale to start your collection. Using a Spitfire as a reference, we can safely assume the 3:2:1 size comparison, meaning that in the space required by a 1/32 scale Spitfire, you can fit two 1/48 scale kits, or three 1/72 scale kits.

Cost is also a consideration. The larger the kit, the higher the initial costs involved, not only for the kit itself, but the amount of consumable materials that you will use such as paint and glue, and, of course, your time.

Before we continue, we must consider the complexity of the model in relation to our own physical limitations and experience. While 1/72 scale is an ideal size for successive projects and relatively low costs, the parts are very small and often require the use of magnification, especially for those of us no longer in our youth. As the scale increases, so does the complexity of the sub-assemblies, the total number of parts and the time required to add them to the model. Historically, many modellers find 1/72 too small and 1/32 too large, so they fall into that heavily populated area of 1/48 scale. In 1/48 and 1/32 scales, the availability of aftermarket detail sets means that even a basic kit can turn into an extensive, and expensive, project. Ultimately, it is up to you to decide (Fig. 1.1).

Finally, we must come to terms with technology. For older modellers, the kits of our youth are still readily available and at reasonable prices. Be warned, however, that many of these older generation kits from the 1960s and 1970s are not the well-fitting, highly detailed kits we once thought they were. They aren't bad; they're simply a product of their time. Do not be tempted by the low prices, as the 1965 Spitfire kit simply does

Fig. 1.2 Vintage kits, although nostalgic, are not always up to modern engineering standards. Often available for bargain prices at shows and swap meets, they can be a perfect way to build skills.

Fig. 1.3 Kits range from low-cost entry level to high-cost expert, but the average kit is generally no more expensive than dinner and a trip to the cinema.

not compare to the 2018 kit (Fig. 1.2). With the advent of computer design, CNC machining and modern manufacturing processes, the old releases from our youth cannot compare to their modern counterparts. This is where a simple Internet search can yield a wealth of information on the kit, its accuracy, level of detail, ease of assembly and cost (Fig. 1.3). Be mindful in your search for a kit, of reissues. Reissues are vintage kits in new boxes, often with modern price tags. Most model company websites provide descriptions of their kits, including whether or not the kit is a new tool or reissue.

There are also dozens of dedicated scale modelling websites with thousands of online kit reviews, offering insight into the project long before you open the box. In virtually all instances, your homework has already been done in the form of online 'sneak peeks', in-box reviews and actual feature-length project builds (Fig. 1.4). Keep in mind, though, that online reviews are written by a wide array of modellers and it is not unusual to find contradictory information about the same kit.

Following are various other considerations to take into account when starting out on your modelling hobby.

PATIENCE

If you talk to any experienced modeller, one of the first things they'll tell you is that this hobby demands patience. In the past, it was possible to buy a kit and have it painted and 'flying' within a few hours. Today, many of us still build with this same subconscious mindset – get it finished, on the shelf and move on to the next project. However, if you are in a rush to see how the model is going to look finished, the chances are this will compromise the quality of the model. Patience is critical. Understand each step of the process and treat each component of the model as if it were the model. Building a quality model is not a race. Like anything else we do in life, it requires planning, thought, patience and

Fig. 1.4 While popular British subjects continue to be released, companies have also started moulding more obscure subjects. Although a Lancaster and Spitfire are obvious choices, an American Liberator in the China–Burma–India theatre is not your average RAF model.

work. A useful strategy, especially with larger, more complex kits, is to finish a sub-assembly completely, including paint and weathering. Although it may seem illogical to the construction process and the kit instructions, it allows the builder actually to finish something in a timely manner and provides the motivation to continue, knowing that eventually all of these components will come together as a finished piece.

ARTISTIC LICENCE

If you have been around the hobby for any length of time, you will inevitably run into all sorts of people, as in everyday life, who see things differently than you do. Modelling is no different. Where you decide to fit, if you choose to fit at all, is ultimately up to you, as this is your *hobby*, your *model*, your *art*. A model is a miniature representation of an actual plane, tank, or ship, at a single moment in time. An aircraft on the day it was delivered has a very different appearance than the same aircraft six months later, but it is nevertheless the same aircraft. At one point in time, everything is new, clean and with pristine paint. Where you choose to position the 'snapshot' of your model is entirely up to you. Most modellers weather their models, making them appear used. Some push those limits and make their models look broken down and war-weary. Other modellers prefer the 'showroom' look, with no weathering at all. Many modellers want absolute historical accuracy, right down to the proper colour of dirt on the undersides because, yes, the dirt at Biggin Hill is a different colour to the dirt at Duxford! There is no right or wrong and the majority of modellers tend to fall in the middle of the two extremes, which, ironically, is where we tend to find the average amount of dirt, grime and wear and tear of an operational combat aircraft.

Always remember – there will never be a 'perfect' model, regardless of how hard you try. Never lose sight of the fact that this is a hobby, for your enjoyment. If painting your Spitfire in the colours of your favourite football team makes you happy, do it. In the end, your happiness is what ultimately matters. Your stance on artistic licence

will change as you build knowledge and experience, as you acquire more references and interact with other modellers who share their knowledge, techniques and resources. Every modeller looks back on their previous work and sees room for improvement. When you finish that first model, it will be your crowning achievement. But there will be errors, omissions, mistakes and inaccuracies. Each new model is a learning experience and an opportunity to apply what you have learnt from the previous one in order to create yet another personal masterpiece. Do not be too hard on yourself, though. If your work is not on a par with everyone else's, figure out why and work to achieve similar results. It will be frustrating, but the rewards far outweigh the struggles.

So you have a kit selected and have prepared yourself mentally to build your best model so far. There are a few more steps in the process before you start building, so let's cover some often overlooked subjects.

REFERENCES

Scale modelling requires research and study. Perhaps not initially, when your sole purpose is to build a model and have fun, but eventually you will run into questions that cannot be answered by the kit instructions. Before the Internet, modellers relied on personal reference libraries for their information and, despite the advances in technology and information access, even beginner modellers are inexorably drawn towards gathering reference books to support their projects. There are general information books that, aside from learning the history and lineage of a specific aircraft, do not really offer much in the technical sense. There are historical references, squadron and unit histories, that, in conjunction with the physical operations of the group, offer period photos of aircraft that can be used as marking references, weathering references and so on. The final type of reference is the technical reference, which is the most beneficial reference to the scale modeller, as it delves into the nuts, bolts and rivets of the actual aircraft. There are thousands of references in all varieties of

Fig. 1.5 Access to information will make your model-building project easier. Some of the print references used in this title are fifty years old.

subjects, aircraft-specific, camouflage application and development, operational histories, modern-day restorations of vintage aircraft, and even the photo-driven 'coffee table' books, whose close-up photos can provide a wealth of information to the modeller (Fig. 1.5).

Today, the average modeller has only to type a few lines into an Internet search engine, such as 'Spitfire Mk.II Merlin engine', and hundreds of photos magically appear, providing the builder with a wealth of instant information. Regardless of your methods, paper or electronic, researching your model and answering those questions ensures that you're putting your best into your art. For many modellers, researching a unique paint

scheme or a lesser-known variant of an aircraft is as exciting as the actual model, as you're not only educating yourself; you're connecting with your work on a much deeper level.

As you spend more time online sourcing references for your model, you will inevitably find scale modelling websites, and there are dozens, some with a specific focus, others more generalized. These sites can be a tremendous asset to the beginner modeller, as they contain kit reviews, feature build stories, conversions, and hundreds of like-minded modellers, all accessible with a click of a mouse. Be warned though – you can spend more time online reading about modelling than actually building!

Chapter Two

Tools, Paint and Chemicals

Now it's time to prepare your tools and work area. Although veteran modellers will often possess every possible tool imaginable, the simple truth is that a good model can be built with a minimum of tools. A hobby knife with no.11 blade, some sanding sticks, putty, cyanoacrylate (super) glue, liquid cement, quality paintbrushes and the various colours of paint you need are all that's required to build a decent model. Remember – quality tools are an investment and, if taken care of, will last for decades.

If you do not have a dedicated work area, select a location that's well-lit and out of the way of pets, children and spouses. The ability to leave your work on the bench while you're away from the project is critical – it prevents parts loss and it won't interrupt the build process by forcing you to pack and unpack your project each time you work on it. It might not seem like a big deal at the moment, but later on in the project you will understand the logic (Fig. 2.1).

TOOLS

The bane of all model builders is not having the right tool for the job, especially when it's most needed. Like anything else we do in life, having the right tools makes the job easier, improves our efficiency and adds to the overall quality of the product we create. If you're starting in the hobby and intend to stay with it, the collecting of tools should be almost as important as the construction of the model. Although it sounds intimidating, many of the advanced tools that modellers use can often be found around the house – it's simply a matter of collecting them and having them readily available (Fig. 2.2).

BASIC TOOLS FOR GETTING STARTED

Following is a list of the basic tools required when starting your modelling hobby:

- hobby knife with no.11 blade
- a few quality paintbrushes
- sanding sticks of various grits
- basic paint colours and thinners
- sprue cutters/nippers
- liquid cement (MEK)
- cyanoacrylate (super) glue
- cotton buds
- masking tape
- small scissors

A few must-have tools should be procured, including a pair of sprue cutters (Fig. 2.3). These are simply fine-pointed wire cutters and can be found in hobby shops, craft stores and beading shops. Though not included in the list, a razor saw is an extremely useful tool, not only for removing or cutting parts, but also as a scribing tool (Fig. 2.4). These saws are available online and through most hobby retailers. A good hobby knife, scribing tools and surgical and dental tools are all useful items for cutting, scraping and general hobby mayhem (Fig. 2.5).

If you are a dedicated aircraft modeller, a riveting tool will be a necessary item, primarily for

Fig. 2.1 A well-organized workbench, with tools and paints easily accessible, makes the hobby much more enjoyable.

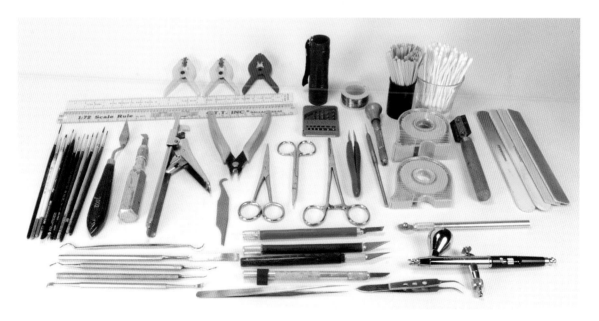

Fig. 2.2 A collection of quality tools is necessary for quality work. The menacing object next to the blue sprue cutters is a tool specially designed to open paint bottles. Although certainly not a requirement, it is a nice tool to have on hand.

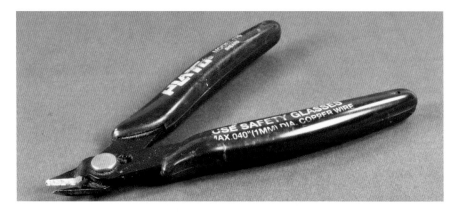

Fig. 2.3 Sprue cutters are a must-have tool for your workbench. The back side of the tip provides a clean, flat cut – perfect for removing parts from the sprues without damaging them.

Fig. 2.4 A razor saw is not mandatory, but serves as an excellent scribing tool in addition to making clean, precision cuts in plastic. The photo-etched blades feature extremely fine teeth.

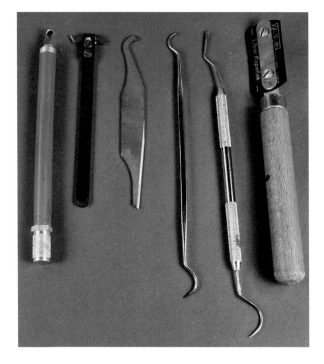

Fig. 2.5 Scribing tools become essential when details are sanded off the model during assembly. They come in a variety of forms, including ultra-sharp knife blades, purpose-designed tools, dental tools and razor saw blades.

One Hundred and One Uses

Miscellaneous items around the house can be helpful in modelling. Here's a quick list of items you can use:

- bottle caps – perfect for mixing small amounts of paint or holding a few drops of cyanoacrylate glue

- straight pins – placed in a hobby knife blade, straight pins make excellent glue applicators

- clothes pegs – great for clamping small parts while gluing, as well as holding parts while painting

- rubber bands – perfect for clamping fuselages while gluing

- scraps of wire – telephone wire, copper wire from discarded electronics and solder wire are ideal for replicating hoses, fuel, brake and hydraulic lines

- pencils – a no.2 pencil is perfect for replicating worn metal; coloured pencils are excellent for weathering

- pastels – work nicely when applied with a brush to replicate exhaust, rust, dust and dirt

- toothpicks – good glue applicators

- craft sticks – perfect for stirring paint

- sticky notes – ideal for disposable paint and glue palettes and simple paint masks when spraying

- fishing line – especially in small sizes, monofilament is perfect for antenna wires

- candle – not for the ambience, but for stretching sprue

- permanent marker pens – great for marking seams

- paper towels/paper napkins – because you will make a mess

- glass cleaner – works well for cleaning parts and brushes

- glass containers – for mineral spirits or other petroleum-based liquids used for cleaning brushes and tools

- storage drawers – ideal for storing spare parts

- pill bottles – perfect for storing small parts, drill bits, hobby blades

- lighter/matches – for the candle

- magnifying glass – because sometimes an OptiVISOR (see below) is not enough

- flashlight – because you will drop parts on the floor and spend hours on your knees searching for them

- tape – masking tape is especially handy not only for masking, but also for test-fitting parts

- squirt bottles – perfect for water, glass cleaner, acrylic thinners

- cotton buds – literally have 101 uses on their own …

- small ruler – so you can measure up

- pliers – to open stubborn paint jars.

replacing details sanded away during construction. There are numerous fixed-wheel types (Fig. 2.6), or the photo-etched variety, which fits nicely into a hobby knife handle (Fig. 2.7).

There are countless tools available around the house that can benefit the modeller. A pair of fingernail clippers works well for removing small parts from sprues; toenail clippers, for larger parts. Cuticle scissors, clothes-pegs, rubber bands, sewing needles, toothpicks, craft sticks, cotton buds, napkins, small bits of wire, and bottle caps, all have a purpose on the workbench.

In addition to items found around the house, as your skills increase you will require more specialized tools. These specialized tools are not always obvious, but they certainly have their uses – surgical haemostats, jeweller's files, small drills, a pin vice and eventually a motor tool. Every modeller should have a hair dryer on hand as well, especially if you choose acrylic paint. Each modeller is unique and each will have a specific set of tools used on a regular basis.

Fig. 2.6 Like scribing tools, rivet tools are needed to replace details sanded off during assembly. The teeth on the wheels create uniformly spaced indentations to replicate flush rivets.

Fig. 2.7 Rivet tools come in a variety of types, but one of the most effective is the Rivet-R from RB Productions. Individual wheels allow for an array of rivet patterns and it fits into a no.5 hobby knife handle.

Paintbrushes

A quality paintbrush is to the modeller what a hammer is to a carpenter, something you must have in order to do your job. Regardless of whether you intend to airbrush your models or hand-paint them, quality brushes are the one item on which every modeller should never compromise. A cheap brush will inevitably yield poor results, while a quality, red-sable brush that is properly cared for can last years. Any good art supply store will stock high-end brushes, and it's a good idea to have a variety of sizes on hand, from 4/0 brushes for ultra-fine detail work, to a no.20 brush for applying washes and filters (Fig. 2.8).

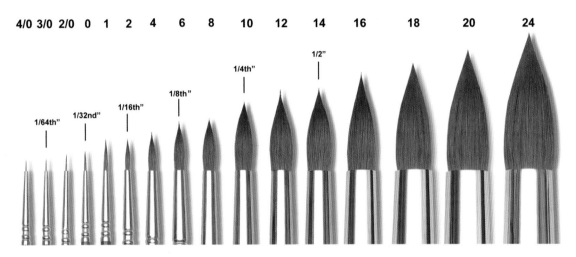

Typical Round Brush Sizes

ABOVE: *Fig. 2.8 Round brushes are the most common variety used in modelling, with modellers using no.10 and down most often.*

RIGHT: *Fig. 2.9 Choose your weapon – a variety of blades serve a variety of roles, such as slicing, chopping, shaving and scraping. You will always have a favourite – the wooden handled knife shown here is made from a piece of teak decking from the battleship USS Missouri.*

Hobby Knives

Although the fancy gift box of fifty different blades and twelve different handles is certainly alluring, the truth is that you are going to use the standard no.11 blade 98 per cent of the time. You can certainly get by with a single hobby knife, but having more than will prove to be an advantage. Hobby knives come in several varieties, from the basic aluminium stock handle to ergonomic handles made from space-age polymers. Like most of your tools,

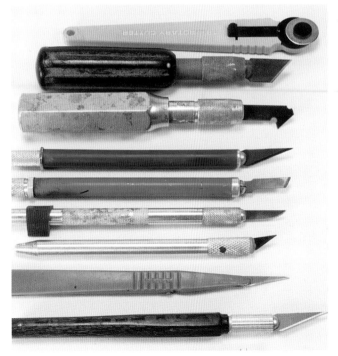

it's a matter of personal preference and you will no doubt have your favourites (Fig. 2.9).

Magnification

Unless you have perfect close-up vision, chances are you're going to need magnification. Avoid the fancy magnifying light fixtures – the novelty wears off as soon as your neck and lower back start to ache. The best all-round tool for the modeller is the OptiVISOR. These headband magnifiers are produced by Donegan Optical and come in a variety of optical strengths and sizes. There are other manufacturers out there, with the quality ranging from very good to very poor. Be mindful of your magnification – it will see extensive use (Fig. 2.10).

Airbrush

Perhaps the largest and most important purchase of your modelling career will be an airbrush. In

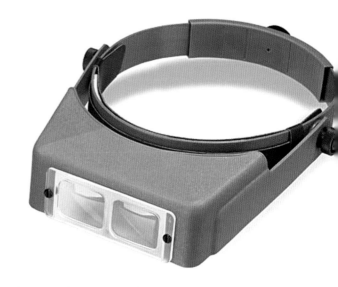

Fig. 2.10 The OptiVISOR by Donegan Optical is perhaps the most overlooked tool on the bench, but it is an absolute necessity when modelling, especially in smaller scales.

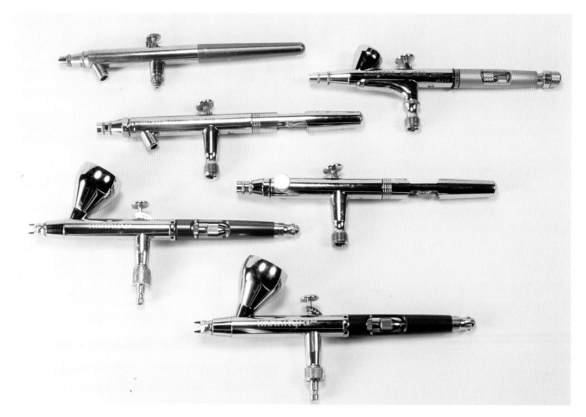

Fig. 2.11 Your largest investment will be an airbrush. Over time, you will find that you start collecting them for specific purposes.

truth, any model can be built without one. The air-brush, however, does what no paintbrush can; a superior, uniform coat of paint and the ability to blend colours and soft edges. Airbrushes range in cost from questionably low to ridiculously high, but, inevitably, you get out of your investment what you put into it. If you choose to start with a basic airbrush, you will eventually find the need for a better unit as your skills increase and you develop advanced techniques such as pre- and post-shading. If you choose to buy the best you can afford, you will eventually grow into the capabilities of the tool, but could be frustrated by the initial learning curve (Fig. 2.11).

Airbrushes come in two basic forms – single and double action. A single-action airbrush is essentially a refined spray can; press the trigger and a uniform mix of paint and air is applied to the model. Single-action brushes are affordable, easy to maintain, offer predictable results and are simple to operate.

A dual-action airbrush retains the constant airflow of the single-action brush, but allows the modeller to adjust the paint flow. This allows for minute applications of paint on to the subject, which is ideal for camouflage patterns, soft-edge demarcation lines and tonal layers of paint for weathering and contrast purposes. Dual-action brushes are generally more expensive and require a bit more practice to master. The dual-action air-brush is, however, the proverbial 'tip of the spear' in modelling tools.

Both types of airbrushes come in three varieties: gravity feed; side feed; and bottom feed. Gravity-feed brushes have a paint cup on the top of the brush and gravity draws the paint into the feed chamber where it is mixed with air and forced through the tip of the brush, which atomizes the paint (Fig. 2.12). Side feed holds paint in a removable cup and feeds the brush using both gravity and the vacuum created by the airflow. Many higher-end types allow the

Fig. 2.12 The Harder & Steenbeck Infinity CR is a high-end, dual-action airbrush perfect for fine detail work.

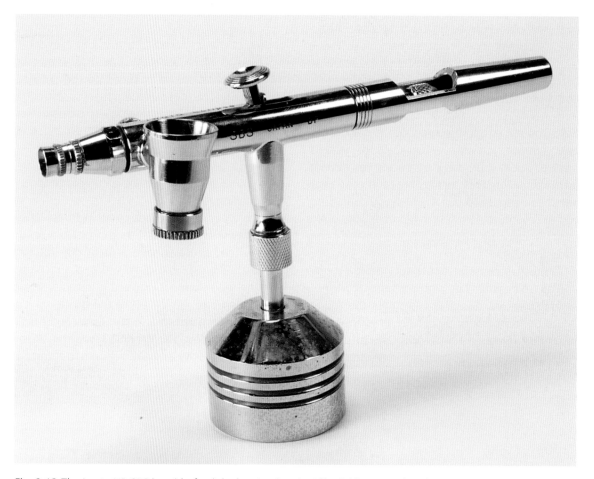

Fig. 2.13 The Iwata HP-SBS is a side-feed dual-action brush. Affordable, rugged and easy to maintain, the Iwata Eclipse series of brushes is well-liked in the scale modelling community.

cup to be positioned on either side of the brush, providing some ergonomic benefit to left-handed modellers (Fig. 2.13). A bottom-feed brush utilizes a paint jar or detachable cup and draws the paint upward by creating suction from the airflow (Fig. 2.14). Each variety of brush has its pros and cons, and each requires a specific set of skills to master. Gravity-feed brushes are ideal for fine detail work with minute amounts of paint; whereas a bottom-feed brush requires a relatively large amount of paint, at least from a modelling perspective, in the jar.

If you have an airbrush, you will need an air source. Most modellers use an air compressor, ranging from small units designed specifically for airbrush use, to large industrial compressors. With a compressor comes the need for a regulator to control the amount of air to the brush, a hose to connect the compressor to the brush and a moisture trap to catch water vapour in the air line. There are countless combinations of brushes and compressors, regulators and hoses; enough, in fact, to write a complete volume just on airbrushing. Keep in mind, however, that unlike industrial spray guns, an airbrush works best between 8 and 15psi of air pressure and the goal is to have small amounts of paint, often not more than a few drops, precisely applied to the model. An airbrush should be considered a scalpel, not a broadsword.

Regardless of what airbrush you choose, proper care and maintenance of your brush will guarantee years of use (Fig. 2.15).

ABOVE: *Fig. 2.14 The Iwata HP-BCS is a suction-feed brush utilizing a detachable paint cup or jar, shown here. This is a very common first-choice for modellers, being affordable, rugged and well suited to general modelling.*

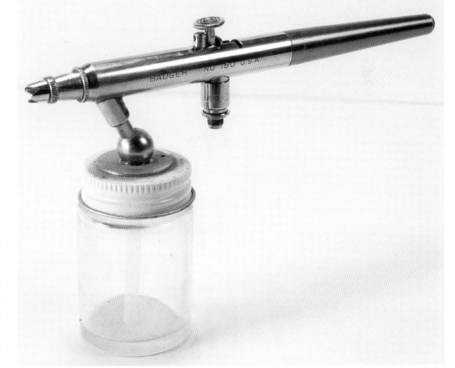

Fig. 2.15 A quality airbrush will last for years if properly cleaned and maintained. This Badger 150 airbrush has been in continuous use since the early 1980s.

Tweezers and Haemostats

The handling of small parts, at least those smaller than your fingers can effectively manipulate, is best handled by tweezers and haemostats, also known as Kelly clamps (Fig. 2.16). Although any bargain-priced pair could work, this is actually one of the most overlooked tools on the bench. Tweezers should have flat-edged, matched mating surfaces, with no lateral movement as you apply pressure. Any lateral movement, or poorly matched surfaces, and your part invariably flies across the room! High-quality tweezers can be sourced online and in the electronic components industry, where handling small resistors, capacitors and circuits is common-place. Kelly clamps, or haemostats, are available in most hobby shops, online and in pharmacies and medical supply stores. These are essentially very small, precise pliers and can be used in a variety of ways, from clamping parts together or gluing to hold parts for painting. They come in a variety of sizes and shapes.

Sanding Sticks

Nearly all good hobby shops will stock sanding sticks and having a variety of grits and shapes is always helpful. If you don't have a hobby shop

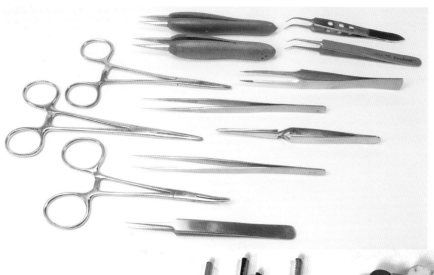

Fig. 2.16 Specialized tweezers from the electronics industry and Kelly clamps from the medical world. These allow modellers to have a firm grasp on whatever they pick up.

Fig. 2.17 Sanding sticks can be sourced not only from the hobby shop, but beauty supply shops and pharmacies as well.

Fig. 2.18 Specialized polishing sticks can be used for everyday modelling, but are best kept for repairing damage to clear parts such as canopies.

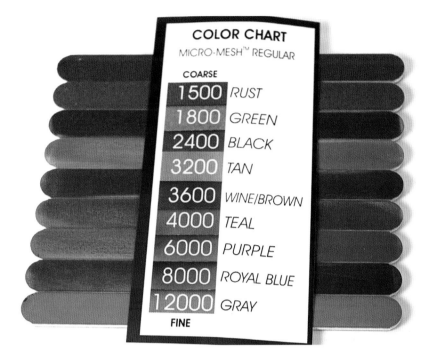

nearby, visit your local pharmacy or beauty supply store – you will find the ladies have cornered the market in fingernail sanding sticks (Fig. 2.17). Although considered an advanced purchase, a set of polishing sticks with very high grits (5,000 and above) is a good item to have on your bench specifically for use with clear parts (Fig. 2.18).

Sandpaper

Sanding sticks are not always the solution to your problem and, sometimes, you need sandpaper. Sandpaper comes in two varieties, woodworking and automotive. In 99 per cent of scale modelling work, automotive Wet and Dry paper is the best option. Available in most hardware and auto-parts stores, Wet and Dry paper is exactly what it says it is, paper designed to be used with water. Wet sanding definitely has its advantages, including no dust and no clogged-up sandpaper. It comes in 8.5 × 11 sheets and in grits from

RIGHT: *Fig. 2.19 Wet and Dry sandpaper from 3M Corporation is available in hardware and auto-supply shops. A variety pack, shown here, features sheets of various grits and can last for months, even years.*

80 for serious sanding to 2000 for polishing. A variety pack of six to eight sheets will last for months of solid model building (Fig. 2.19).

First-Aid Kit

Inevitably, after spending enough time with hobby knives, needle files and cyanoacrylate glue, you're going to need a first-aid kit. It is wise to keep a small one close by to deal with any contingencies that may arise. As a professional modeller, your author has sliced fingers, glued fingers and removed hobby knives from his foot, thigh and forearm. Hopefully you will never need it, but a first-aid kit is good to have around the shop. Ironically, cyanoacrylate glue was actually invented during World War II and has been used as a way to close wounds. There are several companies currently marketing sterilized versions of cyanoacrylate glue for that specific purpose.

Even the most experienced professional modeller won't have every tool or gadget, but starting out with the basics and keeping a keen eye on the hardware store, art supply shop and the cosmetics section of your local chemist can provide you with a wide array of everyday tools that are very helpful in the scale modelling arena.

PAINT AND CHEMICALS

You will need to source paint, as every externally visible part of your model will be painted. There are dozens of brands and three basic types of paint – lacquers, enamels and acrylics. Consideration should be given when you decide on a specific type of paint, as they all have their pros and cons. In the early days, the hobby was dominated by lacquer paints. As environmental and health concerns started to grow, acrylics have gained momentum and now dominate the hobby (Fig. 2.20).

Lacquers are not as common in the hobby as they once were, but most specialized finishes, such as 'metalized' finishes, are lacquers. Lacquer-based paints require lacquer thinner, demand superior ventilation and the use of a respirator mask. Lacquers are the most volatile of the three paint types, so proper and safe ventilation is critical. Lacquer paints spray very well, cover nicely

Fig. 2.20 Just a sample of the paints, glues and fillers used in modelling. Determining which works best for you is a matter of trial and error.

Pros and Cons Chart of Paints

Type	Pros	Cons	Thinner
Acrylics	Water-based, easy to work	Fragile, doesn't bond to plastic	Water or water/alcohol blend
Lacquers	Excellent coverage, durable finish	Fumes, requires superior ventilation	Lacquer thinner
Enamels	Good coverage, bonds with plastic	Fumes, longer drying times	Paint thinner

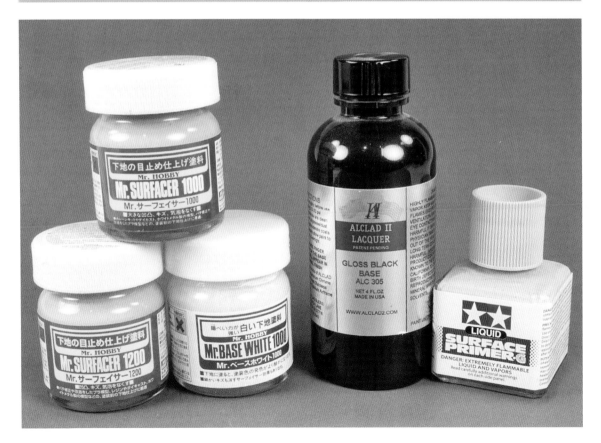

Fig. 2.21 Primers specifically designed for the hobby industry include standard grey and white in bottles and jars, specialized primers like Alclad's black base for metalized finishes and Tamiya's brushable surface primer.

Fig. 2.22 Colour call-outs in kit instructions should always be taken with a hint of scepticism. Generalized terms like 'Dark Green' or 'Dark Grey' can cover an endless spectrum of colours.

and provide a durable finish once cured as they bond with the plastic at a molecular level. Lacquer paint is very aggressive and will melt plastic if applied too heavily. It will also attack underlying coats of other types of paint if applied too thickly.

Enamels require thinning with mineral spirits and they tend to have an odour, so adequate ventilation is a must and the use of a respirator mask is recommended. Enamels take a bit longer to dry, but are resilient to handling once they have cured properly. Because styrene plastic is petroleum-based, enamels also tend to bond to the plastic at the molecular level.

Acrylics thin with water or an alcohol/water blend, dry faster than enamels, but are not as durable, as they do not bond to the plastic on a molecular level. Acrylics are generally water-based, but adequate ventilation and the use of a paint mask is always a safe course of action. The key to good adhesion with acrylics is the use of a primer coat underneath. Primers come in a variety of colours and types. Automotive primer, thinned and sprayed through an airbrush, works nicely, as does primer specifically manufactured for the hobby industry (Fig. 2.21). Avoid generic 'rattle-can' primers, as the pigments are often very thick and the volume of paint is always too heavy.

Your model kit will have colour call-outs (Fig. 2.22). These are usually located in the instructions and indicate what colours are required to complete the model. Kits will include generic colour call-outs, but most kit manufacturers have aligned themselves with paint manufacturers and provide specific numbered colours from a specific brand. Tamiya model kits call for the use of Tamiya paint colours, Airfix references Humbrol colours, Revell references its own line, while Hasegawa references the Japanese Gunze Sangyo line. There are multiple sources for cross-referencing specific colours from various manufacturers including an extensive section in this volume, so once you choose a line of paint that works for you, stick with it.

A consideration for choosing a paint line should also be the availability of subject-specific colours. While one company might offer a generic 'Dark Green', another might offer 'WW2 RAF Dark Green', formulated specifically for your model. Names given to a specific colour by a manufacturer can be misleading. Sky, the standard underside colour of early RAF aircraft, was also called Sky Type S and Duck Egg Blue. Modern iterations of this colour are sometimes called Beige Green, Underside Blue-Green and Sky Green! Model companies will reference these modern iterations of colours, often adding to the confusion. Fortunately, all paint manufacturers offer colour charts of their current lines and, although a US standard, many paint colours have been retroactively approximated to the FS595C paint standard, utilizing a five-digit number to identify specific shades. In addition, the German RAL colour standard offers a variety of choices to help colour match. Keep in mind, however, that both the FS and RAL systems offer specific shades and in some instances do not precisely match vintage colours. In most cases, a close approximation is sufficient, especially when factoring scale effect, washes and weathering. We also have to remember that historically, military paints were produced by dozens of manufacturers, so variations inevitably exist.

Of course, there will come a time when you cannot find a specific colour of paint. As you spend more time in the hobby, you will start to collect paint shades from other nations and often these colours are the exact same mix of paint, but simply wearing a different country's label.

Be prepared at this point – paint, although a consumable product, should also be an investment. If the bottles are properly cared for, they can last for years. If the newly established work area is permanent, factor in a place to store your paint bottles, preferably in a cool, dry, environment. Don't scrimp on paint – we've all seen exception-

PAINT BOTTLE CARE

Paint bottles, regardless of type, should be shaken and kept mixed periodically. This will ensure that the paint doesn't settle and harden in the bottle. It's also wise to clean the rim of the bottle before closing it after use.

ally well-built models ruined by poor paint. If a paint bottle starts to show signs of deterioration, don't risk using it on your model.

UNDERSTANDING THE BASICS

Learning a specific task, be it gluing a model together or learning to tango, requires a combination of pre-emptive knowledge, experimentation and repetition. Before rushing into a project headlong, let's review some quick and easy lessons for basic model construction. Although it may sound obvious, knowing what techniques to use, and when to use them, is your first step into the world of scale modelling.

Fig. 2.23 Liquid cement is available from nearly all major manufacturers of hobby supplies …

Gluing Parts Together

Back in the 'old days' of scale plastic modelling, we had tube cement. We would glue parts, wait hours for them to dry, get light-headed and silly, and generally make a mess of whatever we were working on at the time, not to mention getting glue on Mum's kitchen table. Today's experienced modellers have dispensed with the old tube cement and moved on to adhesives that are much more effective. Scale plastic modelling today relies upon cyanoacrylate (CA), or superglue, and liquid cement, usually a chemical derivative of methyl ethyl ketone, or MEK.

The gluing of wings and fuselage halves is best accomplished with the use of liquid cement, which comes under a variety of brand names but is essentially the same chemical, methyl ethyl ketone (Fig. 2.23). The most common brand in scale modelling since the early 1990s has been Tamiya Extra Thin Cement, but other products include Tenax 7R, Plastruct, Ambroid ProWeld, Testors and Revell Contacta Cement. In truth, most professional modellers buy MEK at their local hardware or paint supply store. In most instances, a quart of industrial MEK is the same cost as 2oz of 'hobby' cement (Fig. 2.24). It is highly recommended that you read and review all of the Safety Data Sheets (SDS; UK, EU), or Material Safety Data Sheets (MSDS;

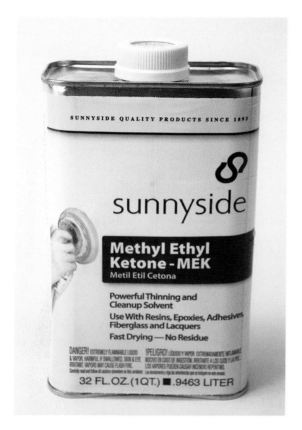

Fig. 2.24 … but a quart-sized can from the hardware store is about the same cost.

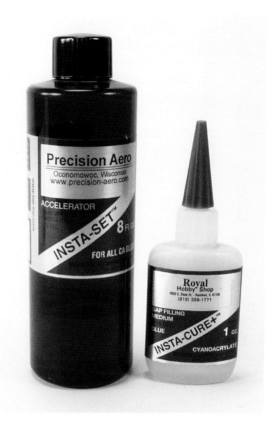

Fig. 2.25 CA glue and accelerator. These two products revolutionized the hobby of scale modelling in the 1980s.

USA, Canada), before using any chemicals you are not familiar with.

Liquid cement creates a solid bond by melting plastic on adjoining surfaces. This is easily achieved via capillary action between the two surfaces. The application of liquid cement can be done directly to the parts, or through the use of a shim between them, allowing the cement to flow along the seam, thus minimizing the chance of a mishap. In the event that liquid cement winds up on a part of the model it's not supposed to, simply allow it to dry without touching it. In most instances, bonding fuselage or wing halves together requires only a few minutes of mild pressure to keep the seam closed; within five to ten minutes the parts can usually be sanded and cleaned up.

Liquid cement is also effective when joining non-structural parts, as the small amounts required to bond the parts minimize the risk of too much glue damaging the model, a problem all modellers have faced, especially in the early days of the messy tube cement.

Cyanoacrylate, or CA, glue for modelling purposes, is overkill in terms of adhesion properties, but it's the gap-filling properties and rapid drying times that have made it popular with modellers (Fig. 2.25). CA requires a specific set of instructions for its use, in particular the handling and application of the glue. CA is especially useful for structural parts and assemblies that are weight bearing, such as landing gear to fuselage, wheels to struts, and wings to fuselages. CA is also useful when parts refuse to cooperate, or in areas that require additional structural strength. The most important rule regarding CA is to *never apply it directly from the bottle or tube*. Instead, apply a few drops to a palette and use a toothpick, wire, or other thin applicator to place a very small amount of glue on to the parts being joined. Allow those parts to dry for several minutes before handling.

CA typically comes in three viscosities – thin, regular and thick. Thin CA has little practical use in scale modelling, as the drying time is too fast and the viscosity so thin that it tends to become messy and difficult to handle. Regular CA is best suited to our hobby and is the typical variety seen outside of scale modelling. Thick CA is almost a gel and is well suited for gap-filling, especially when combined with CA accelerator. Accelerator works with all types of CA, initiating a chemical reaction that causes the glue to dry instantly. CA used in conjunction with accelerator has become a popular method of filling seams. Be warned that the use of CA accelerator in conjunction with CA glue causes a chemical reaction that generates heat proportional to the amounts of chemicals being used.

Contact between CA glue and accelerator on the skin can result in burns. Care should be taken to avoid contact with your skin and always read and understand the warning labels on the package.

Cleaning Up Seams

Once parts are glued together, a quick inspection should be done to determine what degree of work is necessary to fill the seams between the two parts. The cleaning up of a seam requires the filling of any gaps between the two parts and this can be accomplished with putty, glue, or a combination of both based on the severity of the gap. The key to seam-filling is to minimize the damage to the surface of the model along the join.

Modelling Putty

Good styrene putty is a must-have chemical on the workbench, although with a little practice and some alternative methods, you can minimize

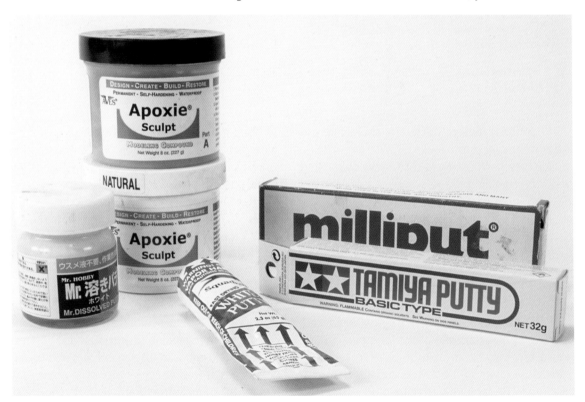

Fig. 2.26 A selection of putty is always good to have on hand, including very thin, dissolved putty for tiny imperfections, standard modelling putty for everyday use and two-part epoxy putty for heavy-duty needs.

its usage as your skills improve over time (Fig. 2.26). Putty is used to fill the seams between two adjoining parts, such as fuselage halves, upper and lower wing halves, or along the wing root where the upper wing mates to the fuselage. Styrene putty is usually a liquid or paste version of the same styrene that a kit is made from, so it softens the plastic of the model and bonds at a molecular level. Apply putty sparingly, allow it to dry fully and sand smooth.

In addition to styrene-based putties, there are other varieties entering the market that are acrylic and clean up with water. Although not as durable as styrene-based fillers, these acrylic fillers are fast, efficient and eliminate the need for aggressive sanding. We will touch upon the use of one of these fillers later on.

There are other types of putty that can be used to fill seams, backfill areas, or add mass. The most common types are two-part modelling putties, such as Milliput or Aves Apoxie Sculpt. Simply mix equal amounts of parts A and B and pack the putty into the area requiring filling. This putty is easy to work with and in the case of Aves and Milliput, clean up with water and a cotton bud.

Modellers should also have white glue (PVA) on hand, for a variety of reasons. White glue offers a bond that is removable, doesn't interact chemically with the plastic and is ideal for attaching clear parts such as canopies and windscreens. White glue is also handy for attaching canopies and other parts for painting, as they can be easily removed after the paint dries. White glue is also a simple solution for the issue of decal 'silvering', which we will discuss later on.

There are dozens of brands of paint, glues, putty and other chemicals that will be used in the creation of a scale model. Some brands will be more accessible than others based on your geographic location; Humbrol and Colourcoats, for example, are far more common in the United Kingdom than in the United States, but nearly impossible to find in Japan. Don't be afraid to experiment with paint brands, as each has its advantages. Some brush well, others are airbrush only. Some require proprietary thinners, some work with a simple water and isopropyl alcohol mix. Find what works best for you!

We've covered just about everything, so now it's time to get to work.

Chapter Three
Hawker Hurricane Mk IIc, 1/48 scale Hasegawa

Every journey begins with a first step, and there's no better first step in modelling than the Hasegawa 1/48 scale kit of the Hawker Hurricane, No.3 Squadron, June 1941. Although this model kit first appeared in the late 1990s, it is still quite relevant in terms of engineering and dimensional accuracy and certainly captures the look of this iconic aircraft. Although there is a seemingly endless supply of aftermarket accessories for this particular kit, a basic out of the box build offers a striking model with a modicum of

effort. Since there is no 'magic formula' to creating a superlative scale model, it is a matter of understanding the instructions and applying a series of experimental techniques until you discover something that suits your preferences (Fig. 3.1).

Developing a system of construction doesn't always follow the instruction path to the letter. Over time, you will develop your own methodology of building and the kit instructions will serve more as a parts placement guide. To that

Fig. 3.1 Box art for Hasegawa Hurricane IIc by legendary box art artist Shigeo Kioke.

end, this kit is a quick and effective way to start your journey.

The kit is moulded in grey plastic and, like the majority of model aircraft kits, construction starts with the cockpit area. The canopy is moulded as a single piece integral with the windscreen, so the canopy will be mounted to the model in the closed position. With this in mind, the cockpit was assembled according to the instructions and sprayed with Tamiya RAF Interior Green XF-71

(Fig. 3.2). A dark brown wash from Ammo by Mig provided some subtle depth and contrast to the stark, monotone finish. The instrument panel was painted with Vallejo Flat Black, dry-brushed with silver, and the instrument faces each received a drop of Humbrol Clear Gloss to replicate the glass (Fig. 3.3). The cockpit framing, seat and instrument panel were assembled and a set of leftover photo-etched seat belts from the spares bin was added (Fig. 3.4).

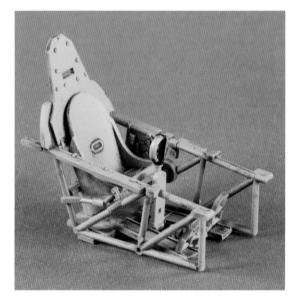

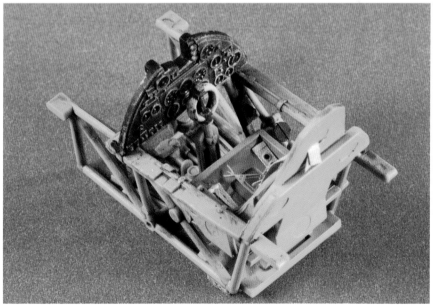

CLOCKWISE FROM TOP LEFT:
Fig. 3.2 The cockpit structure is simple yet effective and looks great with a touch of wash to highlight contrast.

Fig. 3.3 The instrument panel is a simple affair, dry-brushed with silver. With the canopy closed, it is nearly impossible to see.

Fig. 3.4 The completed cockpit assembly. The only aftermarket parts used were a set of photo-etched seat belts.

Fig. 3.5 Apply the Ammo by Mig wash over the bare paint and allow it to dry for a few minutes …

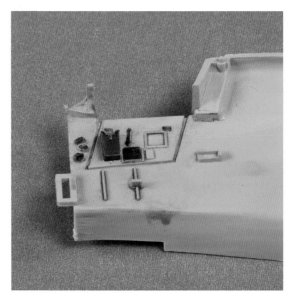

Fig. 3.6 … then remove the excess with a cotton bud and detail the sidewall fittings with black paint.

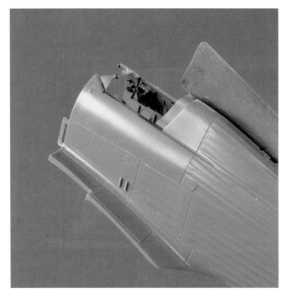

Fig. 3.7 The fuselage halves are joined using liquid cement and a gap-gauge shim.

Fig. 3.8 The fuselage, cannon inserts for the wings and horizontal tail surfaces were puttied with Tamiya Basic Putty and allowed to dry.

The cockpit sidewalls were painted Interior Green, given a brown wash and allowed to dry (Fig. 3.5). As a model size decreases, so does the contrast created by the details of the model, so in most instances fine details are lost. Washes and highlighting create artificial shadows and contrast and bring those details to the forefront, making them 'pop'. Although it appears messy initially, removing the excess with a cotton bud leaves the dark wash in the recesses and provides depth (Fig. 3.6).

The cockpit assembly was installed in the fuselage halves and Tamiya Thin Liquid Cement was applied to the joint with the assistance of a thin metal shim taken from an automotive spark plug gap gauge. The metal shims allow the liquid cement to be applied without marring the plastic. The cement follows the metal shim via capillary action and when applied to both sides of the shim, allows the plastic on each side to be softened. When the metal shim is removed a few seconds later, the result is a near-perfect seam requiring a minimal amount of cleaning up (Fig. 3.7).

With the fuselage halves joined and the nose section attached, the wings were assembled using the same methods and later joined to the fuselage. The balance of the assembly was remarkably simple and quick, as the parts fit very well. Tamiya Basic Plastic Putty was applied to the seams and allowed to dry (Fig. 3.8). After a few hours' drying time, the seams were wet-sanded using 3M Wet and Dry paper in decreasing grits, starting with

400 to remove the heavy material, 600 to shape and smooth, and 1500 to polish the surface. Once satisfied with the quality of the joints, the cockpit area was packed with tissue paper and sealed with masking tape and the model sprayed with Gunze Sangyo Mr. Surfacer 1000 and allowed to dry overnight (Fig. 3.9).

The dawn of a new day saw the model in the home-stretch and the primer was lightly scrubbed with a dry paper towel to remove any residual paint. At this point in the process, the model should be examined and any flaws in the finish and any partially filled seams attended to. If needed, sand the primer and respray. Be patient, and remember, any flaws you see in the primer will be twice as noticeable once your colour coat is applied!

Satisfied with the overall construction quality, it was time to move into the painting process. At this point, most experienced modellers deviate from the logical progression of the instructions. Small parts, such as antenna, landing gear, props, machine-gun barrels, pitot tubes and underwing

Fig. 3.9 After sanding the seams, the model was sprayed with Mr. Surfacer 1000 primer.

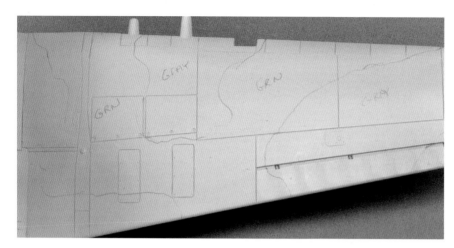

Fig. 3.10 The camouflage demarcation lines were drawn on to the model with a pencil.

Fig. 3.11 The model was sprayed with multiple light coats in a random pattern within the lines to replicate a patchwork appearance in the paint.

Fig. 3.12 The leading edge stripes were masked and sprayed yellow, then the decals applied.

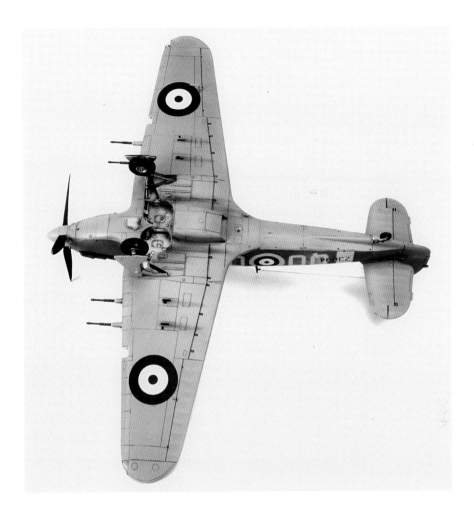

stores are all left off the model. Each of these sub-assemblies will be addressed once the fuselage and wings are painted and drying.

Within the kit instructions you will find both colour call-outs and camouflage scheme diagrams for your particular aircraft. In most instances, this information is usually sufficient for the average modeller, but it's never a bad idea to cross-reference your specific aircraft with outside information, be it a reference book or simple Internet search. In the 1970s, a well-known model manufacturer printed its camouflage data backwards in the instructions, resulting in thousands of incorrectly painted models!

After the camouflage design scheme was matched against official RAF design sheets found online, the demarcation lines were lightly sketched directly on to the surface of the model (Fig. 3.10). The leading edges of the wings and the forward part of the nose were sprayed with Alclad Airframe Aluminium, followed by several extremely light coats of Gunze Sangyo Dark Green and Tamiya Ocean Grey, with the intended goal of making the finish appear war-weary. In reality, the operational wear and tear on an aircraft took its toll on the paint, but ground crews were usually preoccupied with maintaining the mechanical readiness of the craft. By applying thin layers of paint over the aluminium, a degree of fatigue was built into the model, giving it a patchwork appearance (Fig. 3.11). Specific areas around the cockpit were lightly sanded with 2000 grit paper to create the illusion of heavily worn paint with a hint of the aluminium showing through.

Satisfied with the appearance of the paint, but understanding that there was still much more to be done, the wings were masked and the yellow leading-edge stripes sprayed. Because the model was sprayed with gloss colours, there was no need to apply a clear gloss coat on the model and the decals were applied using Gunze Sangyo Mr. Mark Softer, a decal setting solution (Fig. 3.12).

The decals were allowed to dry overnight, giving the setting solution the opportunity to soften the decals and allow them to conform to the compound surfaces of the model and work themselves into the panel lines. A few stubborn decals that refused to cooperate were gently sliced along the panel line with a no.11 blade and setting solution reapplied.

With the decals in place, it was time to blend everything together. Ammo by Mig provided the Blue-Black panel line wash that was applied to the entire surface of the model (Fig. 3.13). It is here, with the application of an ugly, messy, potentially ruinous sludge wash, where many modellers choose to stop the finishing process. The inherent fear of ruining the model at this late stage is actually a detriment, as the overall wash is critical for creating the artificial shadow and contrast, as well as blending all the layers of paint and decals together under a single tonal layer. Fear not, for

once the wash has dried and is wiped away, the panel lines become more prominent and the model develops a uniform sheen (Fig. 3.14).

Experimentation with washes is also a keen idea – removing all of the wash leaves a glossy, uniform finish, whereas leaving traces of residual wash can be used to replicate weathering, oil streaks, gun residue, or other naturally occurring environmental effects. Depending on how much wash you want left on the model determines what you use to wipe it down. If you want to leave a heavier residue on the model, wipe the model down with a dry paper towel or napkin. If you want less residue, use a soft cloth. Regardless of how much wash you choose to leave on the model, it should be wiped down as soon as the glossiness disappears from the surface, generally within five to ten minutes. The longer you wait, the more difficult it becomes to remove the wash. If the wash needs to be

Fig. 3.13 The entire model was coated with Ammo by Mig Blue-Black panel line wash and allowed to dry for fifteen minutes.

Fig. 3.14 The wash was removed with a dry paper towel, in the direction of the airflow. Some wash was allowed to remain on the wings to replicate streaking.

removed completely, a cotton bud dipped in white spirits will remove it.

With the majority of the paintwork done, the fuselage was set aside and allowed to dry for twenty-four hours. This break in the process allowed for the construction of the external sub-assemblies, such as the prop and spinner, landing gear, exhausts and canopy, all of which were built and painted according to the instructions (Fig. 3.15).

The bane of most aircraft modellers is canopies and windscreens. The process of applying paint to clear plastic, painting thin canopy frames and attaching them to the model has frustrated all modellers at some point. Fortunately, the Hurricane canopy is an excellent first-time candidate, as the panels are uniform in their curvature and simple to mask. The quick and easy approach to canopies can be found in pre-cut paint masks, available from an array of manufacturers and designed for specific kits. These masks are quite simple – remove the pre-cut section, attach it to the canopy and spray. But, in the interests of being 'old school', there's a do-it-yourself method that will yield excellent results.

In the world of electronics, specifically within the manufacturing of printed circuits, there exists a specific brand of tape called Kapton tape, manufactured by 3M Corporation. This tape is vinyl, has excellent non-aggressive adhesion properties and

Fig. 3.15 The landing gear, prop and exhaust stacks were all weathered then attached to the fuselage. All that remains are the clear parts and antenna.

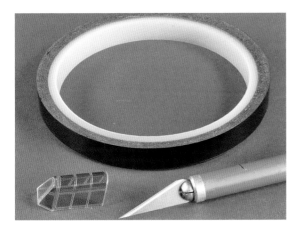

Fig. 3.16 The canopy was masked with 3M Corporation Kapton tape, then sprayed.

Fig. 3.17 The canopy was attached to the model, then lightly sprayed to blend into the fuselage. The entire model was given a coat of Vallejo clear varnish.

can be stretched nicely over compound curves. The real benefit, however, is that it is clear with a gold tint. This allows the tape to be placed and, with a steady hand and a new blade, trimmed to fit (Fig. 3.16). The clear nature of the masking tape allows the canopy to be inspected for any masking imperfections prior to painting.

Satisfied with the masking, the canopy was painted with Dark Green and installed on to the aircraft with the masks still in place (Fig. 3.17). The sub-assemblies were attached except for the landing lights, navigation lights and antenna, and the model given a coat of Vallejo clear flat varnish. This seals everything in place – the washes, the weathering, the decals and the paint.

The final steps in the process involved attaching the clear parts – landing lights, wingtip naviga-tion lights and antenna wire. The clear parts were attached using white glue and the antenna was tacked into position using 2lb monofilament fishing line and CA glue.

Last, the canopy masks were removed and some pigments, or weathering powders, were applied to replicate exhaust streaks, gun residue and a hint of dirt and dust on the landing gear. These were simply brushed on to the model with light strokes and any excess wiped off with a cotton bud.

From start to finish, this model required approx-imately twenty-two hours of work and utilized the following paints, washes and pigments:

- Gunze Sangyo H312 Kfir Green paint
- Gunze Sangyo H73 British Dark Green paint
- Tamiya XF-82 British Ocean Grey paint
- Gunze Sangyo H335 Medium Sea Grey paint
- Gunze Sangyo H329 Chrome Yellow paint
- Alclad Airframe Aluminium paint
- Alclad Burnt Iron paint
- Ammo by Mig – Dark Grey Wash (undersides)
- Ammo by Mig – Blue-Black Wash (topsides)
- Ammo by Mig – Grey-Green Wash (interior)
- Gunze Sangyo H2 Black paint
- Warpigs Mid Rust pigment, Dark Earth pigment, Black pigment.

Sir Sydney Camm's Hurricane seems lost in the shadow of the Spitfire, but was an equally impor-tant aircraft to the RAF, especially during the Battle of Britain, where it accounted for 60 per cent of the RAF victories. Although not as fast as the German Bf-109, it was more manoeuvrable and, in the hands of a skilled pilot, was a formi-dable adversary. As the war progressed and the Hurricane reached its zenith as a fighter, it, like so many other RAF aircraft, was repurposed into other roles, excelling especially in the fighter-bomber role. Fitted with two 40mm Vickers cannon, the Hurricane IID went on to become the RAF's most potent tank killer until the Hawker Typhoon appeared on the scene.

Fig. 3.18 A photo of Z2963 shows the wing gun openings, gun camera and the numerous streaks and fluid leaks commonly seen on operational aircraft. US NATIONAL ARCHIVES

Fig. 3.19 No two cockpits are the same. This is a cockpit of a Hurricane IB from 1940. CANADIAN NATIONAL ARCHIVES

Fig. 3.20 This cockpit is an unarmed Hurricane XII serving with No.1 Naval Air Gunnery School, RN, October 1944. CANADIAN NATIONAL ARCHIVES

Fig. 3.21 The cockpit of Hurricane Z3174, a Canadian-built Mk IIa painted in the markings of 71 Squadron. This aircraft is preserved at the USAF Museum in Dayton, Ohio, USA. USAF

Fig. 3.22 A superdetailer's dream come true – the left side of the cockpit of Z3174. Of special interest are the fuel selection switch, rudder trim and elevator trim controls, complete with bicycle chain and gears. USAF

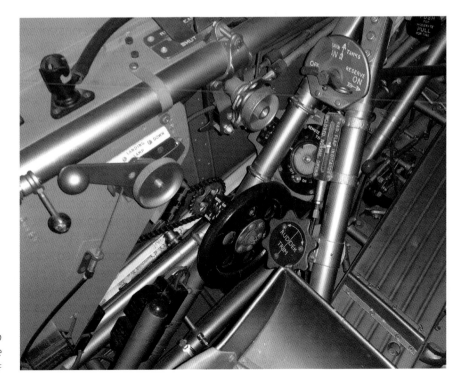

Fig. 3.23 A close-up of the left side of the cockpit. USAF

Fig. 3.24 Hurricane PZ865 was the last Hurricane built. The aircraft is painted Dark Earth and Dark Green, with Medium Sea Grey undersides, and wears the markings of HW840, 34 Squadron, South East Asia Command, 1944. The aircraft is operated by the Battle of Britain Memorial Flight at RAF Coningsby. CPL PHIL MAJOR, RAF/MOD

Fig. 3.25 Hurricane LF363, operated by the Battle of Britain Memorial Flight, is also maintained by that group. This detail shot shows the Merlin engine with the panels removed. Notice the engine exhaust stubs are each a different shape, something commonly missed in model kits. CPL PHIL MAJOR, RAF/MOD

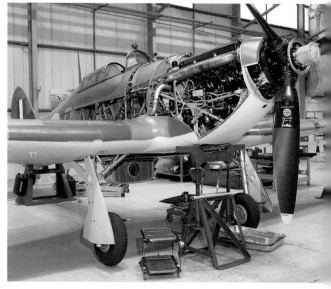

Fig. 3.26 Hurricane LF363 with most of her private parts showing, including the spinner, revealing the constant pitch mechanism of the Rotol prop. CPL PHIL MAJOR, RAF/MOD

Fig. 3.27 Hurricane Mk IIb Z3174 is actually a Canadian-built Hurricane XII, serial number 5390. The aircraft is painted in RAF 71 Squadron markings and carries the standard Day Fighter scheme of Dark Earth, Dark Green and Sky, with underwing roundels. This scheme was in effect from 22 April 1941 to August 1941. USAF

Fig. 3.29 Hurricane P3408, a Mk I aircraft with No.85 Squadron, during the Battle of Britain. IWM

Fig. 3.28 Museum aircraft and warbirds afford the perfect opportunity to photograph specific details. This is Hurricane KZ321 at the EAA AirVenture in Oshkosh, Wisconsin, USA. Notice the control surfaces, elevators, down rudder to one side and trim tabs. Most model kits have control surfaces in perfect alignment. JEFF BARRETTE

Chapter Four

Supermarine Spitfire Mk IIa, 1/32 scale Revell

Spitfire – the name is as legendary as the aircraft. To the scale modeller and aviation enthusiast, it needs no introduction. It is perhaps the most famous aircraft of World War II, certainly from a British perspective. There have been hundreds of iterations of Spitfire models over the years in a variety of scales, but this particular kit, of the Supermarine Spitfire Mk IIa, No. 65 Squadron, May 1941, is the most recent 1/32 scale release of the legendary Battle of Britain-era fighter (Fig. 4.1).

The kit lends itself well to the beginner modeller, but the detail-minded modeller will find a few issues that will require some extra effort and, like most model kits, there's ample room for improvement if the builder so chooses. The sprues are moulded in light grey plastic, while the panel lines and rivet detail are superb. Test-fitting of the major components seems to indicate a very well-engineered kit. This particular model was supposed to be a straight-up, out of the box build targeting

Fig. 4.1 The Revell Spitfire Mk IIa in 1/32 scale. A relatively new kit, this is perhaps one of the most affordable 1/32 kits on the market today.

the beginner modeller. For most modellers, it will fit that bill perfectly, but online research into the kit highlighted some critical accuracy issues and it was decided to address those issues in this build.

Unless your model kit is equipped with an engine, it is highly probable that construction commences with the cockpit area. This model is no exception and the cockpit is reasonably detailed for a kit of this size. Construction starts with the assembly of the floor, forward bulkhead and instrument panel, following the instructions.

After the assembly of the cockpit sidewalls it was determined that the kit parts simply would not do, as they lacked the depth of detail, especially with the canopy slid back and the door open. A pair of resin replacement panels from Aires, designed for the venerable Hasegawa 1/32 scale Spitfire Mk Vb, were utilized (Fig. 4.2). Amazingly, these kit-specific resin parts fit exceptionally well in the newer Revell kit, with only a few millimetres of trimming required from the forward parts of the panels to allow the kit parts to fit (Fig.

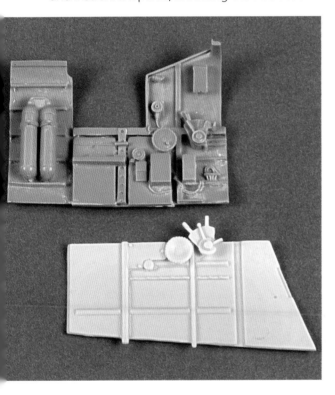

ABOVE: *Fig. 4.2 The cockpit side walls in the kit were replaced with a resin set from Aires. The additional detail is quite obvious.*

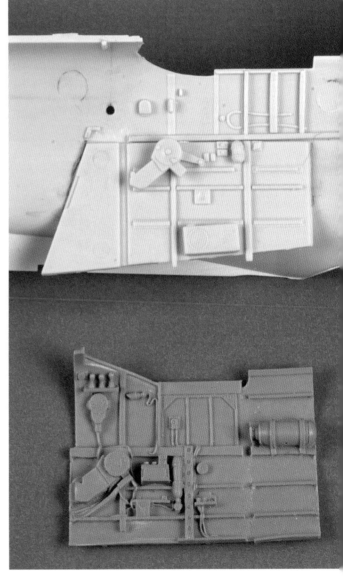

Fig. 4.3 The starboard side cockpit wall. This sidewall is more noticeable if the cockpit door is opened.

4.3). The results are spectacular; the trimming and fitting work was significantly less than the actual assembly of the kit parts and to better effect (Figs 4.4, 4.5).

The cockpit, rudder pedals and instrument panel were glued together and, deciding that an aftermarket instrument panel was going to be used, the kit part was sanded flat. After gluing the floor, rudder pedals and instrument panel parts together (Fig. 4.6), the cockpit components were sprayed with Gunze Sangyo H312 Kfir Green (Fig. 4.7), which is a close match to RAF Interior Green. Perfect tonal accuracy is not always necessary, especially if you intend to enhance the cockpit area with washes and filters to increase the tonal contrast.

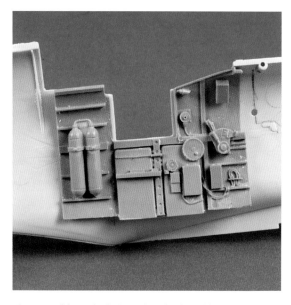

Fig. 4.4 Although designed to fit the older Hasegawa kit, the Aires panels required minimal work to adapt to the newer Revell kit.

Fig. 4.5 Resin detail parts are an added expense, but can save you hours of work if your intention is to add detail.

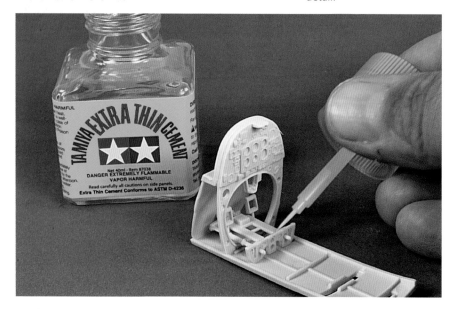

Fig. 4.6 The cockpit floor, instrument panel and rudder pedal assembly were built with Tamiya Extra Thin Liquid Cement.

The next step in the assembly of the cockpit involves the seat and corresponding support structures and bulkheads. A test-fit of the kit seat exposed a serious flaw – the seat was too small. Several seats were pulled from their donor kits, including a vintage Hasegawa seat, a seat from a Pacific Coast Models Mk IX Spitfire and the seat from the Aires resin update set that provided the cockpit sidewalls (Fig. 4.8). Comparison of the seats determined that the kit part is indeed very undersized, so the Aires resin seat provided the best alternative. While focused on the cockpit area, it was decided to replace the cockpit door with a resin replacement part from BarracudaCast (Fig. 4.9). Since the model would have an open cockpit, the resin replacement part offered more

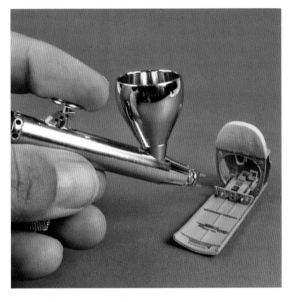

Fig. 4.7 The instrument panel detail has been removed and the assembly given a coat of Interior Green.

Fig. 4.8 The kit seat (far right) was far too small, especially when compared to Pacific Coast Models, Hasegawa and Aires. The Aires seat was chosen as the replacement.

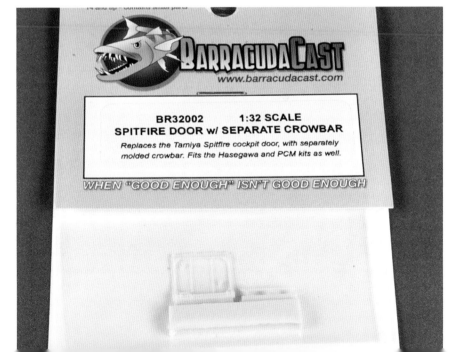

Fig. 4.9 It's all in the details, and BarracudaCast does a superb resin-cast cockpit door, complete with 1/32 scale crowbar, which ironically, was not used on Mk I and II aircraft.

detail than the kit part. The remaining cockpit parts were painted Interior Green, using Gunze Sangyo Kfir Green (Fig. 4.10).

The details of the side panels were picked out with Vallejo black paint (Fig. 4.11), then a Green Brown panel line wash was applied from Ammo

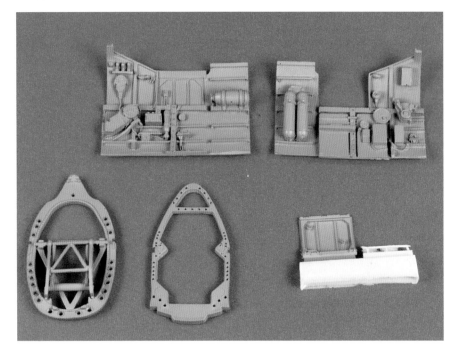

Fig. 4.10 All of the cockpit parts received a coat of Gunze Sangyo Kfir Green, a good baseline match for RAF Interior Green.

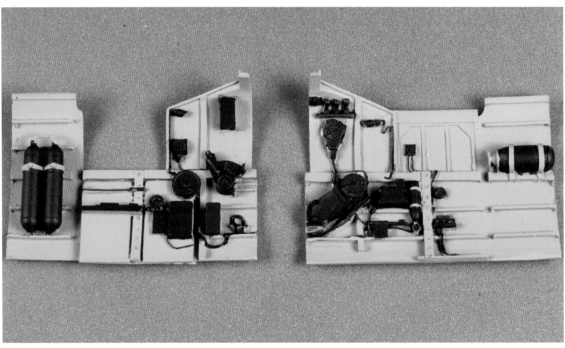

Fig. 4.11 The sidewall details were painted with Vallejo flat black paint.

by Mig (Fig. 4.12) and allowed to dry (Fig. 4.13). The excess was removed with a cotton bud, followed by another Ammo by Mig Dark Brown

wash to the cockpit sides, bulkheads and floor. As the wash dried, it took on a very dirty, oily appearance. A few passes with cotton buds removed the

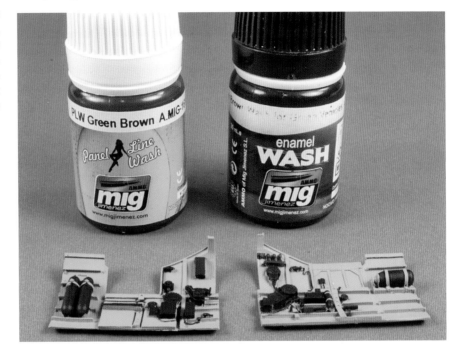

Fig. 4.12 Enamel washes were used to create contrast and depth. Always use opposite types of wash and paint ... in this case, enamel washes over acrylic paint.

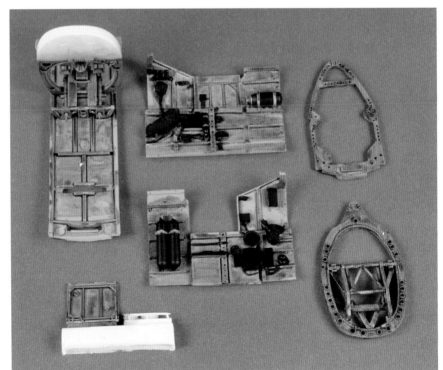

Fig. 4.13 Applying a wash requires absolutely no talent whatsoever – just be sure to get it into all the cracks, crevices and corners.

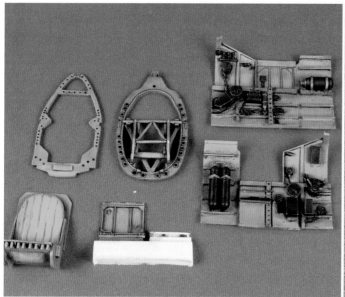

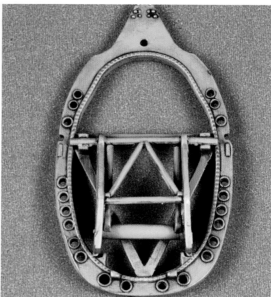

Fig. 4.14 After ten to fifteen minutes of drying time, remove the excess with a cotton bud, leaving the wash in the corners and recesses for contrast.

Fig. 4.15 The bulkhead supporting the pilot's seat shows to good effect what a wash can do to enhance the realism of the part.

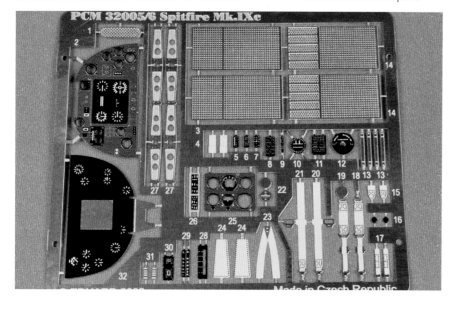

Fig. 4.16 An Eduard photo-etched fret provides details that simply cannot be reproduced in plastic.

excess from the smooth surfaces of the parts and left trace amounts in the recesses and rivet details, providing an artificial contrast that allowed the details to pop (Figs 4.14, 4.15).

One of the most difficult things to master in aircraft modelling is instrument panel details. The kit part is nicely moulded, but painting gauges and dials on the instrument panel requires patience and practice, and is often frustrating. So in the interests of time and detail, the kit panel was sanded smooth and a photo-etched Eduard printed instrument panel installed in its place (Fig. 4.16). The results are fantastic, with a degree of detail that is nearly impossible to replicate with a brush and paint (Fig. 4.17). The balance of the cockpit was assembled – the bulkheads, seat and stick (Fig. 4.18). The seat cushion was painted with Vallejo 875 Beige Brown and a Red-Brown panel line wash applied over the brown. This gives the seat that distinctive brown leather look. Eduard photo-etched seat belts were fitted and the cockpit was ready for installation (Fig. 4.19).

Although only a small portion of the cockpit area is visible once the fuselage halves are closed, Interior

Fig. 4.17 The instrument panel was added in place of the sanded-off kit details and a drop of clear gloss on each instrument gives the illusion of glass.

Fig. 4.18 The completed cockpit tub, ready for assembly into the fuselage.

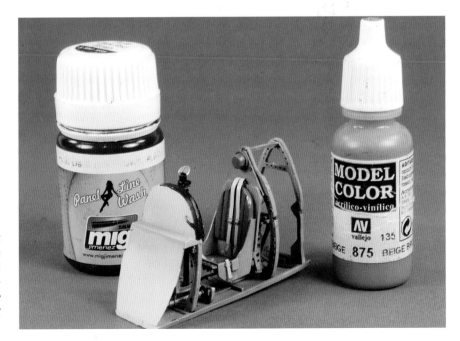

Fig. 4.19 The seat was painted with Vallejo Beige Brown, given an Ammo by Mig Red-Brown wash and the photo-etched seat belts installed.

Green was applied to the interior spaces and the cockpit side panels installed (Figs 4.20, 4.21). The fuselage sub-assembly was test-fitted, then glued to the left side of the fuselage (Fig. 4.22).

Fig. 4.20 The details were touched up, cockpit placards installed and some of the detail parts from the Eduard set.

Fig. 4.21 The stringers on the right side were modified to allow the kit bulkhead to fit.

Fig. 4.22 The cockpit assembly was glued into the left side of the fuselage, test-fitted with the fuselage closed, then glued into place

Fig. 4.23 The wings were assembled using Tamiya Extra Thin Liquid Cement and a spark-plug gap gauge as a shim. The shim draws the cement into the joint without the brush touching the surface of the model and marring the plastic.

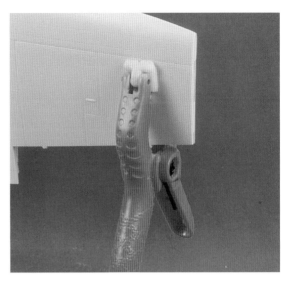

Fig. 4.24 Simple spring-loaded clamps from the hardware store hold the wing halves together while the cement dries.

Fig. 4.25 Perfect Plastic Putty and an artist's palette knife were used to putty the seams of the model.

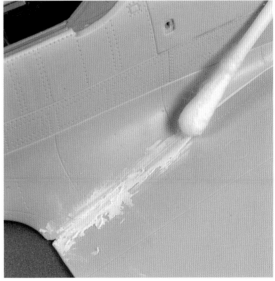

Fig. 4.26 Water and a cotton bud are used to scrub the seams once the putty is dry …

The fuselage halves and wings were test-fitted and Tamiya Extra Thin Liquid Cement was applied using the soon to be patented spark-plug gap-gauge method (Fig. 4.23), allowing for capillary action to bond the surfaces together with a minimal amount of mess. The wings were clamped for a few minutes (Fig. 4.24), then joined with the fuselage and the horizontal stabilizers attached. The model was puttied up using Perfect Plastic Putty and a painter's palette knife, then allowed to dry (Fig. 4.25). After the putty had set for thirty minutes, a wet cotton bud was used to remove the excess (Fig. 4.26). Unlike petroleum-based putties utilized in the past, Perfect Plastic Putty is

water soluble, so removing the excess resolves the wing and fuselage seams without destroying the surrounding details (Fig. 4.27).

The seam at the top of the nose cowling was a bit more pronounced and levelling the plastic with sandpaper was necessary to facilitate a smooth joint. After working on the 'step' between the fuselage halves, putty was reapplied and sanded smooth. The resulting loss of the panel line on the upper cowling required the rescribing of the line. Dymo-brand embossing tape, used in handheld label makers, is a perfect tool for rescribing panel lines (Fig. 4.28). The tape is made of hard plastic, is easily cut to length and provides a perfect straight edge for the rescribing of panel lines (Fig. 4.29). The panel was rescribed using several light strokes

Fig. 4.27 … and the resulting seam is perfect – with no damage to the surrounding plastic.

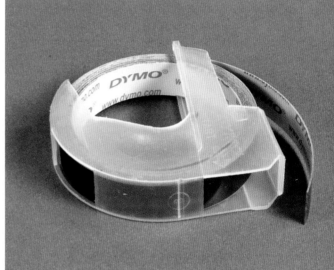

Fig. 4.28 Dymo tape is perfect for rescribing lost panel lines. It is made of a flexible, yet hard, plastic.

Fig. 4.29 The tape is cut into a piece and placed on the model parallel to the panel line.

from an UMM-USA scribing tool (Fig. 4.30) and the rivet detail replaced using an RB Productions tool (Figs 4.31, 4.32).

In preparation for priming, the cockpit was gently packed with tissue paper and sealed with masking tape to prevent overspray (Fig. 4.33). As the tissue was pushed into the cockpit, care was taken not to damage the stick or other various levers, dials and handles already in place. The tissue was moistened with a few drops of water to allow it to conform, then covered over with masking tape.

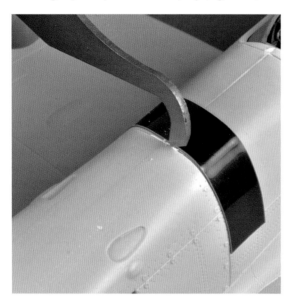

Fig. 4.30 Using the tape as a guide, a scribing tool cuts into the plastic to restore the panel line.

Fig. 4.31 The Rivet-R tool from RB Productions was used along the same panel line to replace the rivets lost to sanding.

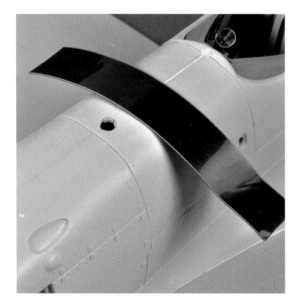

Fig. 4.32 The resulting details are restored and the Dymo tape removed.

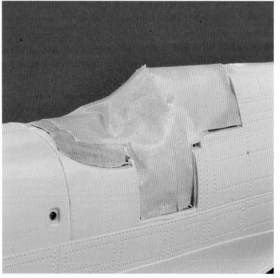

Fig. 4.33 Tissue paper is pressed into the cockpit and moistened with a drop of water to conform to the interior, then covered over with masking tape.

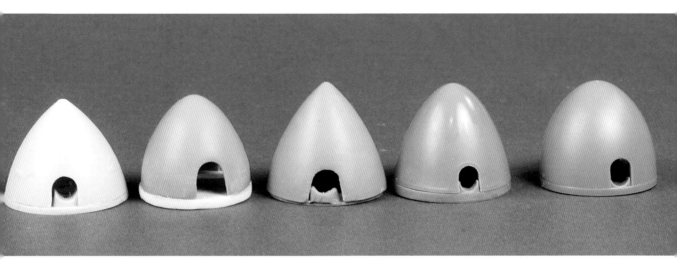

Fig. 4.34 Spitfires carried a variety of spinners, but the kit spinner (left) did not match examples from other kits. Left to right: Revell AG, Revell 1960s, Hasegawa 1980, Pacific Coast Models 2006.

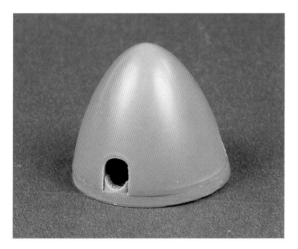

Fig. 4.35 The spinner from the venerable Hasegawa kit was chosen as a replacement, as it best matched the shape of the spinner on the actual aircraft.

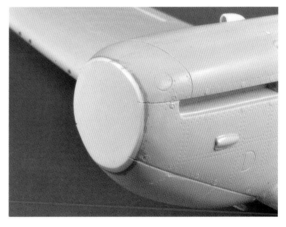

Fig. 4.36 The diameters of the spinners were different, so a piece of styrene was glued to the nose and shaped accordingly, with panel lines and rivets, to match the diameter of the replacement spinner.

The next step in the instructions required the assembly of the spinner, but it was obvious that the kit-supplied part simply did not look right, as it appeared too conical and too short, ruining the graceful lines of the Spitfire's nose. Although Spitfires carried two varieties of propellers and spinners, Rotol and de Havilland, each with their own distinctive spinner shapes, the kit spinner really does not match either, so spinners were taken from several other kits and compared (Fig.

4.34). Ultimately, the spinner from the venerable Hasegawa Spitfire Mk II kit was chosen as the replacement, as it most accurately matched the various line drawings being used as reference (Fig. 4.35). The diameters of the two spinners were different, and after again referencing line drawings, a piece of sheet plastic was cut to rough shape, glued to the nose, sanded smooth and panel lines extended with a razor saw (Fig. 4.36). This created the proper nose diameter, resolved what appears visually to be a too short nose, and provides an excellent mating surface for the Hasegawa spinner. The spinner backplate was aligned to the nose and marked, then a hole drilled into the nose to accommodate the propeller shaft. The model was sprayed with Gunze Sangyo Mr. Surfacer 1000 and allowed to dry (Fig. 4.37), providing the opportunity to work on the sub-assembly parts, including the landing gear, prop blades, spinner, exhaust and wheels.

Modellers inevitably test-fit their parts, often long before it's necessary, and although this was no different than any other build, a test fit did reveal another slight flaw in the kit, albeit a very minor one. Like a crooked picture frame on a wall, sometimes even the slightest discrepancy

can catch a discerning eye and it was the height of the main landing gear wheels that seemed off. After consulting references to verify that Spitfire wheels were in fact uniform in size, the kit wheels were compared to wheels from other kits and found to be small, so a replacement set was taken from a Spitfire XIV resin conversion set containing three different sets of wheels. As Spitfire wheels appeared in three-, four- and five-spoke varieties, the five-spoke wheels from the resin set were deemed surplus to an upcoming Spitfire project and procured for this one. A dry fit reveals a better stance and the resin wheels possess a slight flat spot to replicate a bit of weight (Fig. 4.38). The wheel hubs were sprayed with silver (Fig. 4.39), then a circular vinyl mask placed over the hub to

LEFT: *Fig. 4.37 The model was sprayed with Mr. Surfacer 1000 and set aside to dry.*

BELOW LEFT: *Fig. 4.38 The kit wheels (left), simply did not look right, so a resin replacement set from a Mk XIV conversion set was substituted. The size difference is obvious.*

BELOW RIGHT: *Fig. 4.39 The wheel was drilled for use as a holder and the centre hub sprayed silver.*

cover the centre section (Fig. 4.40) and pressed into place (Fig. 4.41). The tyre was sprayed (Fig. 4.42) and after the black paint had dried, the mask was removed to reveal the finished wheel (Fig. 4.43).

Fig. 4.40 A circular vinyl mask was used to cover the hub …

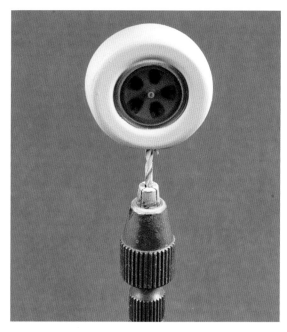

Fig. 4.41 … pressed into place …

Fig. 4.42 … and the wheel painted flat black.

Fig. 4.43 The mask was removed to reveal a perfectly painted tyre and wheel.

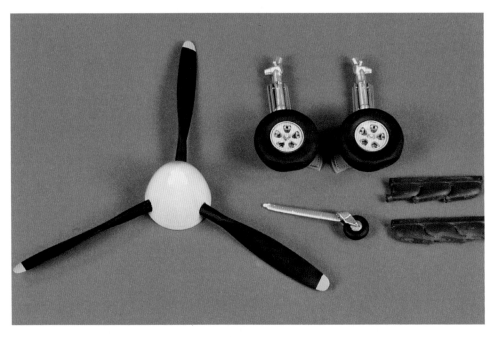

Fig. 4.44 The remainder of the 'easily broken while handling' parts were assembled and painted.

The remainder of the sub-assemblies were built and painted, including the prop, landing gear legs, tailwheel and exhaust. Each was painted according to the instructions and set aside (Fig. 4.44).

With the sub-assemblies complete, it was time to get back to the fuselage, which by this time was fully cured and ready for paint. The model was wiped down with a dry paper towel, to remove any residual primer and smooth the surface for the paint coat.

The masking and painting of a camouflage pattern is a tedious process, determining the accurate location of each boundary of colour, working around compound curves and raised details and avoiding overspray. In the past, modellers have relied on a variety of methods, from regular masking tape and liquid masking products, to a combination of non-modelling products such as Silly Putty, Blu-Tack, newspaper and sticky notes. A fellow modeller, whilst on an extended stay in hospital, discovered Microfoam medical tape by 3M Corporation (Fig. 4.45). This tape is specifically used for holding IV lines and other medical devices in place after surgery. It is flexible with excellent adhesion properties, does not chemically react with paint and is very easy to apply and manipulate. Fortunately, it is available in most pharmacies and online.

The kit instructions were scanned into a computer, enlarged to 238 per cent, then printed (Fig. 4.46). Since kit instructions vary, enlarging them

Fig. 4.45 A new discovery, 3M Microfoam medical tape, is ideal for masking models.

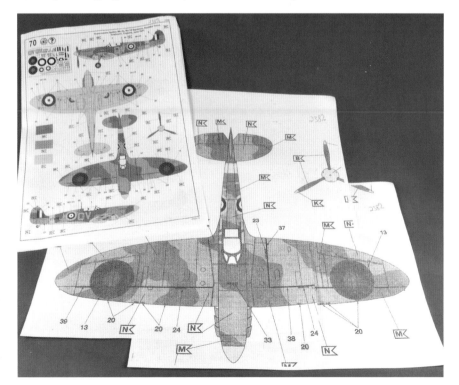

Fig. 4.46 The painting guide in the kit's instructions was scanned, then enlarged, in this case to 238 per cent to match the size of the actual model.

is simply a matter of trial and error until the templates in the instructions match the actual model. The Dark Earth portions of the pattern were cut out (Fig. 4.47), then used as templates to cut the shapes from the Microfoam tape (Fig. 4.48). The model was free-sprayed with Gunze Sangyo H74 British Dark Earth on the upper surfaces (Fig. 4.49) and Gunze Sangyo H75 Sky on the undersides (Fig.

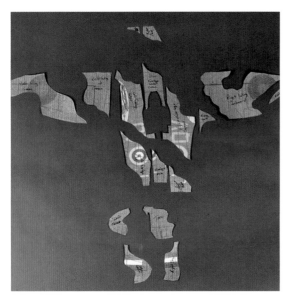

Fig. 4.47 Each of the Dark Earth portions of the pattern were cut from the enlargement and labelled.

Fig. 4.48 Each piece was then used as a template to cut corresponding masks from the Microfoam tape.

Fig. 4.49 Gunze Sangyo H74 British Dark Earth was applied to the upper surfaces and allowed to dry.

4.50) and allowed to dry. The masks were fitted to the model and sprayed with Gunze Sangyo H73

British Dark Green (Fig. 4.51). Amazingly, when the masks were removed, the result was a near-

Fig. 4.50 The model was free-sprayed with Gunze Sangyo H75 Sky and allowed to dry.

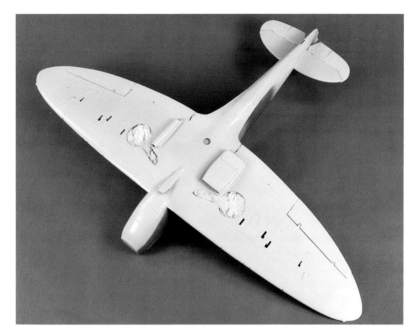

BELOW: *Fig. 4.51 The Microfoam masks were applied over the Dark Earth, then Dark Green was sprayed on to the model.*

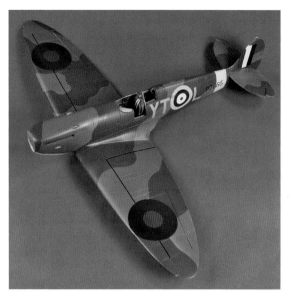

Fig. 4.52 The masks were removed to reveal a perfect finish.

Fig. 4.53 The decals were applied to the model using just Micro Set decal setting solution.

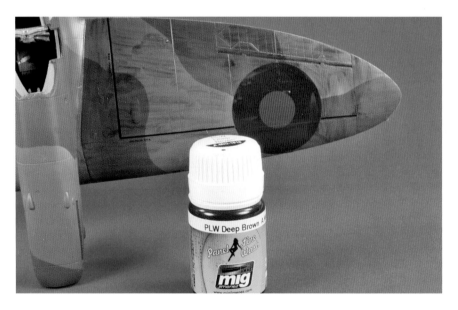

Fig. 4.54 Ammo by Mig provided a Deep Brown panel line wash – perfect for the brown and green tones.

perfect paint scheme requiring no touch-ups (Fig. 4.52).

The decals for the model were allowed to soak in warm water mixed with a few drops of white glue (PVA). This prevents decal silvering, those telltale signs of an air pocket between the decal film and the surface of the model. Although the water evaporates away as the decals dry, the trace amounts of white glue remain, acting as a bonding agent between the decal and the model's surface, and dries clear (Fig. 4.53).

After the decals were positioned, a coat of Micro Sol decal setting solution was applied to soften the decal and allow it to conform to the surface details of the model. This process went remarkably well and after a few hours of drying time,

Fig. 4.55 The panel line wash was wiped down with a dry paper towel, giving the model a uniform sheen and tone.

Fig. 4.56 The 'easily broken while handling' parts were attached to the model. It's starting to look like a Spitfire.

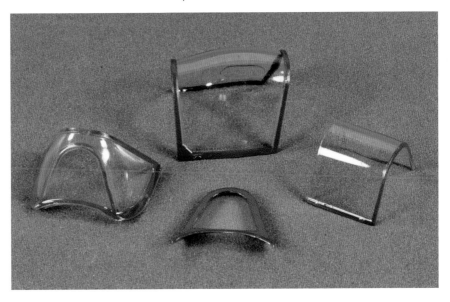

Fig. 4.57 The clear parts were masked with Kapton tape and sprayed with Dark Green.

the model was covered with an Ammo by Mig Deep Brown panel line wash (Fig. 4.54). The wash was allowed to dry for approximately ten minutes, then wiped away with a dry paper towel. The resulting residual wash left behind in the recesses, rivets and panel lines serves to provide depth and contrast to the model (Fig. 4.55). Based on photos of the actual aircraft, the weathering and overall wear and tear on this particular model was kept to a minimum. At this stage in the process, the sub-assembly parts were attached to the model, except for the canopy (Fig. 4.56). The clear parts were masked with 3M Kapton tape and sprayed, allowed to dry and the masks removed (Fig. 4.57).

The model was sprayed with a light coat of Vallejo clear flat varnish, the clear parts attached

Fig. 4.58 The finished model is a fine representation of the Spitfire.

and the antenna wire rigged using 4lb mono-filament fishing line painted black. After the construction of the model was deemed complete, exhaust streaks, gun residue and a slight trace of earth tones were added to the model with pigments. These dry powders were simply lightly brushed on to the model, then the residual wiped away.

This particular kit, despite a few technical inaccuracies, is well engineered, easy to build and, in the end, looks every bit the iconic Battle of Britain Spitfire. Total time on this model was nearly forty hours, with roughly 25 per cent of that time dedicated to the cockpit, 25 per cent dedicated to fixes and upgrades, and the remaining 50 per cent to construction and painting (Fig. 4.58).

The following materials were used on this model:

- Gunze Sangyo H312 Kfir Green paint
- Gunze Sangyo H73 British Dark Green paint
- Gunze Sangyo H74 British Dark Earth paint
- Gunze Sangyo H75 British Sky paint
- Gunze Sangyo H329 Chrome Yellow paint
- Alclad Airframe Aluminium paint
- Alclad Burnt Iron paint
- Ammo by Mig Dark Grey Wash (undersides)
- Ammo by Mig Deep Brown Wash (topsides)
- Ammo by Mig Grey-Green Wash (interior)
- Gunze Sangyo H1 Black
- Warpigs Mid Rust pigment, Dark Earth pigment, Black pigment.

Entire volumes have been written on the Spitfire, from the first prototype to the last of the line, the F.24, and some will even include the Seafang and Spiteful as extensions of this amazing lineage. Today, more than fifty Spitfires are operational, with dozens more on static display in museums around the world. Anyone who sees a Spitfire fly for the first time and hears the Merlin or Griffon as it races past, is gifted with a rare opportunity to witness what many claim, and justifiably so, to be aviation perfection.

Fig. 4.59 Spitfire R7347, a Mk I turned Mk Va, sent to the United States for NACA evaluation at Wright Field, Dayton, Ohio. Of particular interest is the non-standard serial number font and the excessive amounts of oil on the underside of the aircraft. US NATIONAL ARCHIVES

Fig. 4.60 Spitfire MK Ia, serial X4179, coded QV-B, of 19 Squadron, RAF, at Fowlmere, Cambridgeshire, circa 1940. NASM

Fig. 4.61 No one will argue – Spitfires are beautiful. This Battle of Britain Memorial Flight Spitfire, complete with D-Day stripes, is warming up on the ramp in this award-winning photo by Sgt Pete George. This shot was the 2014 Ministry of Defence Photo of the Year. SGT PETE GEORGE, MA/MOD

Fig. 4.62 Cockpit of Spitfire MK Ixe based in Virginia, USA. SHANNON O'NEILL

Fig. 4.63 Cockpit of the Spitfire Mk Vb on display at the United States Air Force Museum in Dayton, Ohio. USAF

Fig. 4.64 An absolutely brilliant photo of Spitfire Mk Vb SN-M of 243 Squadron, RAF. NASM

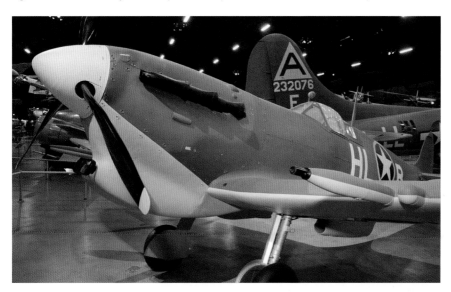

Fig. 4.65 Some might call it blasphemy, a Spitfire in US markings, but it shows to great effect the Volks air filter. The filter performed remarkably well, preventing dirt and dust from entering the engine, but completely kills the aesthetics of the sleek design. USAF

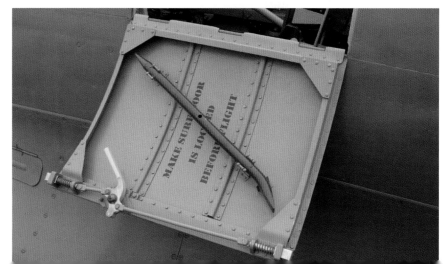

Fig. 4.66 Cockpit door of a Seafire MK XV, a Griffon-powered navalized Spitfire.
JEFF BARRETTE

Fig. 4.67 The starboard side canopy of the Spitfire, showing the emergency canopy release mechanism, another often overlooked detail on Spitfire models. WAYNE DIPPOLD

Fig. 4.68 Excellent wing-root view of a Seafire XV, showing to great effect the panel line inconsistencies. Modellers might demand that their panel lines be perfect, but on the actual aircraft, it is rarely the case, even on highly maintained warbirds. JEFF BARRETTE

Fig. 4.69 Located behind the pilot's seat is the aircraft's voltage regulator. WAYNE DIPPOLD

Fig. 4.70 About to touch down, Spitfire TE311, an LF XVIe, is a low-back, clipped-wing Spitfire. The aircraft was the gate guard at RAF Tangmere for a dozen years before appearing as a 'taxi only' stand-in for the Battle of Britain film in 1968–9. The aircraft was allocated to the RAF Exhibition Flight as a static exhibit until taken in hand and restored to flying condition by the Battle of Britain Memorial Flight in 2012. CPL PHIL MAJOR, RAF/MOD

Fig. 4.71 Stunning photos can still have research value to modellers! This photo, taken by SAC Graham Taylor, was the 2016 Ministry of Defence Photo of the Year. It shows Spitfire TE311 doing a 'hot start'. Despite the beauty of the photo, it shows to great effect the inconsistencies in the panels of the aircraft. SAC GRAHAM TAYLOR, MOD

Chapter Five

Mosquito Mk VI, 1/48 scale Tamiya

Modellers define kits by their accuracy, their engineering and ease of assembly. Not many kits survive more than a decade or so before they are supplanted by a superior kit, with a few notable exceptions. Tamiya's 1/48 kit of the de Havilland Mosquito FB Mk VI, 305 Squadron (Polish), June 1944, is one of those exceptions and has held the distinction of being one of the finest Mossie kits available in 1/48 scale (Fig. 5.1).

This particular project delves into the finishing aspects of the model, as the construction is about as straightforward as one can expect. In fact, this model is built entirely out of the box, with no aftermarket parts of any kind, save for a few strands of wire to connect the radios on the rear deck of the cockpit. Entry and exit of the Mosquito is via a hatch on the lower starboard side of the aircraft, meaning that the canopy is closed. This restricts the ability to see into the cockpit – as a result, extensive detailing is not required, as the majority of it is hidden from view. To that end, the Tamiya cockpit area is well detailed, including decals for the seat belts. Although the purist may choose to use aftermar-

Fig. 5.1 The Tamiya Mosquito has been on the market for twenty years and still remains one of the finest kits of the Mosquito available in 1/48 scale.

ket belts, to all but the keenest eye the decal seat belts do the trick.

The cockpit sub-assembly combines the cockpit area with the bomb bay and wing spars. The four .303 machine guns in the nose offer ammunition bins, but once the fuselage is closed these are hidden from view, so they were left off (Fig. 5.2). The instrument panel was painted black and instrument decals applied. The balance of the cockpit area was painted and given a contrast wash of Ammo by Mig Dark Grey (Fig. 5.3). The underside of the bomb bay was painted RAF

Fig. 5.2 The cockpit assembly is straightforward with no issues. Although a large number of aftermarket parts are available, the kit's parts are more than sufficient once the canopy is installed.

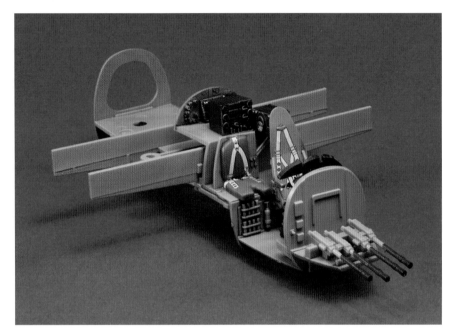

Fig. 5.3 The kit's instrument panel is surprisingly detailed, using the instrument decals supplied with the kit.

Interior Green and the fuel tanks painted in Oxide Red, again according to the instructions (Fig. 5.4). The entire assembly then fits into the fuselage halves using the wing spars as anchor points (Fig. 5.5). The kit provides the bomb-bay doors as a single piece, but the cannon-armed version of the Mosquito utilized a split bomb-bay door, as the forward portion of the bomb bay was occupied by the breaches of the 20mm cannon.

Having painted and detailed the fuel-tank assembly, it seemed a shame to hide it within the confines of the bomb bay (Fig. 5.6), so the

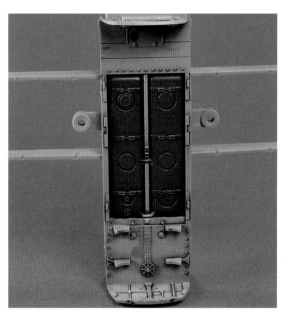

Fig. 5.4 The bomb bay and fuel tanks provide a splash of colour, so it was decided to open the bomb-bay doors. The tanks were painted Oxide Red and given a Blue-Black wash.

Fig. 5.5 The cockpit, forward gun pod, bomb bay and wing spars are all one integral piece.

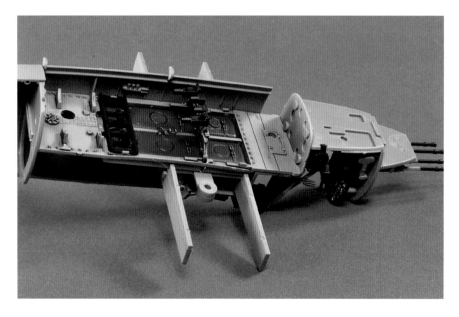

Fig. 5.6 The breaches for the 20mm cannon and the bomb racks were installed prior to closing the fuselage.

doors were cut utilizing a fine razor saw (Fig. 5.7). The fuselage halves were joined together, and the nose section of the fuselage added. The fuselage and wings were assembled according to the instructions, glued, puttied and sanded smooth (Fig. 5.8). The split bomb-bay doors were installed to the underside of the aircraft and the wheel wells, bomb bay and cockpit area were gently packed with tissue paper in preparation for painting (Fig. 5.9).

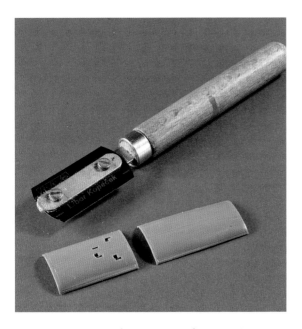

Fig. 5.7 Because the forward part of the bomb bay was occupied by the four 20mm cannon, the doors had to be cut with a razor saw.

Fig. 5.8 The fuselage was assembled and puttied, and the cockpit packed with tissue paper.

Fig. 5.9 The forward half of the bomb-bay doors were installed and the bomb bay and wheel wells were likewise packed with tissue ahead of painting.

Fig. 5.10 The model was given a coat of Mr. Surfacer 1000 primer and wiped down with a dry paper towel after it had dried.

Fig. 5.11 The areas for the D-Day stripes were free-sprayed with Tamiya Gloss White and left to cure for forty-eight hours.

The model received a coat of Mr. Surfacer 1000 primer, allowed to dry, then polished with a dry paper towel (Fig. 5.10). This polishes the surface and removes any powdered residue of paint. This often occurs if the air pressure is too high while spraying as the paint dries before it hits the surface of the model, resulting in a grainy, rough finish. With the model primed and smoothed, Tamiya

Gloss White X-2 was applied to the wings and fuselage in preparation for D-Day invasion stripes (Fig. 5.11). White can be a finicky colour to paint, so the base white was allowed to dry for a full forty-eight hours to ensure it was fully cured.

When the invasion of the Continent was announced in early June 1944, orders had already been prepared for the application of recognition

Fig. 5.12 Strips of Microfoam tape were cut and laid side by side for uniform spacing.

Fig. 5.13 The two interior strips of tape were removed from each wing and the fuselage.

markings for Allied aircraft and the Mosquitoes were no exception. The standard five-stripe configuration of three white and two black stripes, each 18in (457mm) in width, were to be applied to the wings and fuselage. Some units measured, masked and sprayed their invasion stripes, while others used a piece of rope to create a straight edge and applied the stripes with brushes and even mops. Photos of

305 Squadron Mosquitoes indicate their markings were applied with care, as the stripes are uniform in width and position, and the paint well applied, so each of the stripes for the model were cut from 3M Microfoam tape and laid side by side (Fig. 5.12), using each stripe to maintain the proper alignment with the next. Once the stripes were in place, the second and fourth strips were removed (Fig. 5.13)

and Gunze Sangyo Gloss Black H2 sprayed over the open areas (Fig. 5.14). These were also allowed to dry for a full forty-eight hours before they were covered over and the remaining Dark Green, Ocean Grey and Medium Sea Grey colours were applied (Fig. 5.15). After yet another forty-eight hours of drying time,

RIGHT: *Fig. 5.14 Gunze Sangyo Gloss Black was sprayed over the revealed stripes and allowed to cure for forty-eight hours.*

BELOW: *Fig. 5.15 The masks were left in place, the black portions were recovered with tape and the model sprayed with Gunze Sangyo Dark Green and Tamiya Ocean Grey.*

the tape was removed to reveal an almost-perfect paint job, requiring just a few minor touch-ups with a small brush (Fig. 5.16). The kit decals were applied, using only a partial fuselage code, with the rest of the code being 'covered' by the D-Day stripes and a Polish flag decal taken from an RAF Blenheim decal sheet. The markings were applied with Micro Sol setting solution, allowed to dry, then sprayed with clear gloss to seal them (Fig. 5.17).

Fig. 5.16 When the grey and green had dried for twenty-four hours, the masks were removed, revealing almost perfect D-Day stripes.

Fig. 5.17 Decals were applied to the model using Micro Sol decal setting solution.

Fig. 5.18 A Brown-Grey panel line wash from Ammo by Mig was applied to the wings …

Photos and a few online videos of 305 Squadron Mosquitoes seem to indicate that their aircraft were exceptionally well maintained, so this particular model was not heavily weathered. An Ammo by Mig Brown-Grey panel line wash was applied to the wings (Fig. 5.18), undersides (Fig. 5.19) and fuselage (Figs 5.20, 5.21), allowed to dry for five minutes, then removed with a paper towel. Although the wash was subtle, it highlighted the panel lines and acted as a filter, bringing all of the

Fig. 5.19 … the fuselage, including the decals …

Fig. 5.20 … and the undersides.

Fig. 5.21 The wash, despite its dirty appearance on the model, works into the panel lines to create artificial contrast and depth.

Fig. 5.22 After the wash is removed from the model, what remains on the surface reduces the sheen of the paint and puts everything under a single tonal layer.

various colours together under a single tonal layer (Fig. 5.22). The wash was more noticeable on the undersides of the aircraft, effectively breaking up the monotone nature of the underside grey (Fig. 5.23).

The fuselage was set aside and allowed to dry. Despite the various layers having in excess of forty-eight hours' time to cure, once the wash was applied the model was given a full week to sit without handling. This was done in preparation for the final clear coat of flat to be applied, ensuring that everything underneath the last layer of paint was fully cured.

While the fuselage was drying, focus switched to the small parts, such as gear doors, props, spinners, landing gear and canopy. These parts were assembled and painted according to the instructions.

The cannon-armed Mosquito could still carry four 500lb bombs, two on wing pylons and two in the bomb bay. The bombs were assembled, painted Gunze Sangyo H59 IJN Green, which matches nicely to British Bronze Green, given a black wash, scrubbed with a light green pigment and clear coated (Fig. 5.24). The gear doors and bomb-bay doors were painted and washed with the same Brown-Grey

Fig. 5.23 The wash is especially noticeable on the undersides of the model, where the lighter Medium Sea Grey colour has been applied.

Fig. 5.24 The bombs each went through a four-step process. Left to right: Gunze Sangyo H59 IJN Green paint; black wash; black wash removed; light yellow artist's pigments.

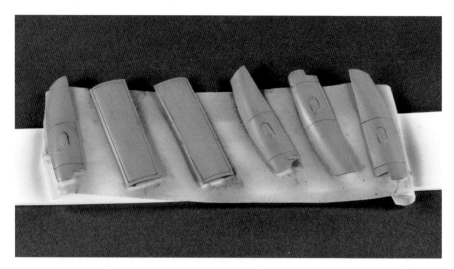

Fig. 5.25 The gear doors and bomb-bay doors were painted and washed with the same shade of Brown-Grey.

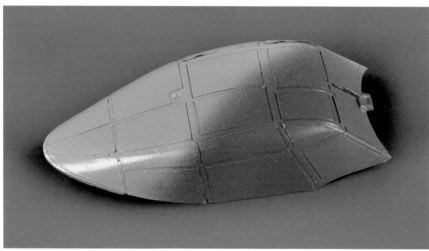

Fig. 5.26 The canopy was masked with Kapton tape and sprayed.

panel line wash (Fig. 5.25). The canopy was masked with Kapton tape and sprayed with black. This creates the illusion that the interior of the canopy frames are painted. The canopy was test-fitted on to the fuselage, the demarcation lines between colours were marked and the canopy sprayed (Fig. 5.26). The small parts were allowed to dry fully and after a week's time all of the sub-assemblies were ready for installation (Fig. 5.27).

The final steps were the installation of the canopy, navigation lights and radio antenna wire. Total time on this model was thirty hours, with ten hours of construction time and twenty hours of painting, weathering and decaling. This kit, despite its 1998 release date, is still the finest Mosquito offered in 1/48 scale. It is extremely well engineered, easy to build and offers tremendous room for super-detailing.

The following materials were used on this model:

- Gunze Sangyo H312 Kfir Green paint
- Gunze Sangyo H73 British Dark Green paint
- Tamiya XF-82 British Ocean Grey paint
- Tamiya X-2 Gloss White paint
- Gunze H2 Black paint
- Gunze Sangyo H59 IJN Green paint
- Gunze Sangyo H335 Medium Sea Grey paint
- Gunze Sangyo H329 Chrome Yellow paint
- Alclad Airframe Aluminium paint

Fig. 5.27 The model ready for final assembly.

- Alclad Burnt Iron paint
- Ammo by Mig – Dark Grey Wash (undersides)
- Ammo by Mig – Blue-Black Wash (topsides)
- Ammo by Mig – Grey-Green Wash (interior)
- Gunze Sangyo H2 Black
- Warpigs Mid Rust pigment, Dark Earth pigment, Black pigment.

Unlike Spitfires and Hurricanes, only thirty-three Mosquitoes remain of the nearly 8,000 built, and although a half-dozen are being restored to flight status, there are only three aircraft in the world currently flying. The remainder of the aircraft are static displays, or in the case of the Mosquito prototype at London Colney, far too rare to risk flying. The Mosquito was perhaps the first truly multirole aircraft, functioning as a bomber, fighter bomber, night fighter, photo-reconnaissance and maritime patrol aircraft. Even though others are compared for their versatility, such as the American B-25 and German Ju-88, at the time the Mosquito was operating, it was the predominant aircraft of its function. When German Ju-88 night fighters were attacking bomber formations, night-fighting Mosquitoes hunted the Ju-88s. When pinpoint tactical bombing was required, it was the Mosquito squadrons that did the job.

Fig. 5.28 Instrument panel of the B.35 Mosquito located at the EAA Museum in Oshkosh, Wisconsin, USA. The aircraft is owned by Kermit Weeks and the Fantasy of Flight Museum and is on long-term loan to the EAA.

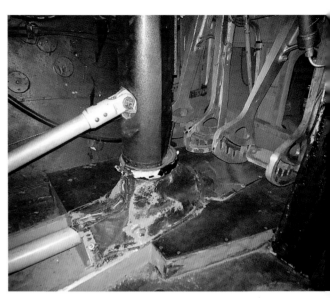

Fig. 5.29 A photo you won't see every day … the rudder pedals and control column attachment point on the fuselage floor. The rudder pedals are adjustable … taking into account the pilot's ability, or inability, to reach them.

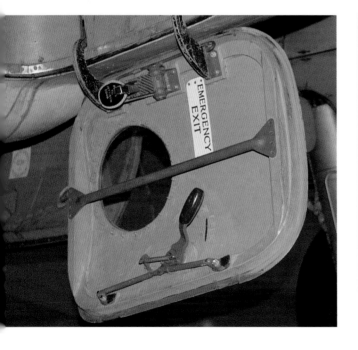

Fig. 5.30 The access hatch, located on the bottom of the aircraft. On fighter and fighter bomber versions, this hatch was located on the side of the fuselage and required a ladder to access. In either version, the Mosquito was not an easy aircraft to get out of.

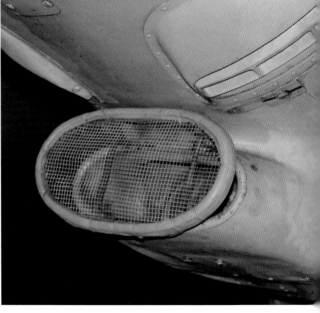

Fig. 5.31 Starboard engine intake with debris screen. This was installed on Mosquitoes to prevent any debris from entering the engine.

Fig. 5.32 Portside flap of the Mosquito. Notice the paint wear on both the upper flap surface and the very end of the engine nacelle.

Fig. 5.33 The tail of the Mosquito. The stencils on the lower part of the tail are positioning stencils for the rudder lock and are marked 'External Control Locking'.

Fig. 5.34 The starboard side of the bomb aimer's position in the nose.

Fig. 5.35 Overall view of the tail and elevator. Paint wear on the horizontal stabilizer and elevator is excessive, yet closer examination reveals that the paint is worn smooth, not chipped or peeling. The only logical explanation can be the effects of the airflow over the control surfaces.

Fig. 5.36 A line-up of Mosquito B.XVI bombers. The XVI used the Merlin 72, which is easily identifiable by six exhaust stacks instead of the typical five. NASM

Fig. 5.37 Mosquito FB.VIs of 487 Squadron, Royal New Zealand Air Force, in close formation. ARCHIVES NEW ZEALAND

Fig. 5.38 Mosquito B.XVI ML963 of 571 Squadron taken in flight, 30 September 1944. NASM

RIGHT: Fig. 5.39 This 143 Squadron Mosquito FB.VI, part of the Banff Strike Wing, banks away from legendary aviation photographer Charles E. Brown's camera in 1945. The photo shows to good effect the weathering on the underside of the aircraft, including the relatively short exhaust stains and repairs to the underside of the portside horizontal stabilizer.

FLEET AIR ARM MUSEUM

Fig. 5.40 Nose section of the Mosquito TT/B.35 held at the Smithsonian National Air and Space Museum in Washington, DC. NASM

Fig. 5.41 Cockpit of the NASM Mosquito. NASM

Fig. 5.42 Mosquito PR.IX MM230 served with 105 Squadron during the war and was struck off charge on 22 November 1946. NASM

Chapter Six
Swordfish Mk II, 1/48 scale Tamiya

This Tamiya kit, of Fairey Swordfish, 816 Squadron, HMS *Tracker*, September 1943, is, like most Tamiya kits, a near-perfect balance of quality engineering, detail and ease of assembly (Fig. 6.1). Tamiya's Swordfish was first released in 1998 as a Mk I aircraft and it was not until 2007 that the Mk II kit was released, albeit with a majority of parts from the original Mk I kit. Although a very well-engineered kit, the Swordfish should not be tackled as a first project, simply because of the aircraft itself – it is a biplane. Biplane aircraft pose difficulties to many modellers due to the nature of the wings. With a monoplane, the primary consideration is the dihedral of the main wings, whereas with a

biplane, you not only have two sets of wings to worry about aligning with the fuselage, but care and consideration must be taken to ensure the alignment of the upper and lower wings as well. Biplanes also carry rigging wires, a detail which can prove as frustrating to experienced modellers as they are to beginners.

The Swordfish was a metal-framed, fabric-covered aircraft with a large, open cockpit area. This means that extra attention is required on the insides of the fuselage halves. The fuselage interior of the Swordfish is a mix of Interior Green, Flat Black and red primer, so the fuselage halves were painted green, then masked, and the fabric

Fig. 6.1 Box art of the 1/48 scale Tamiya Swordfish Mk II.

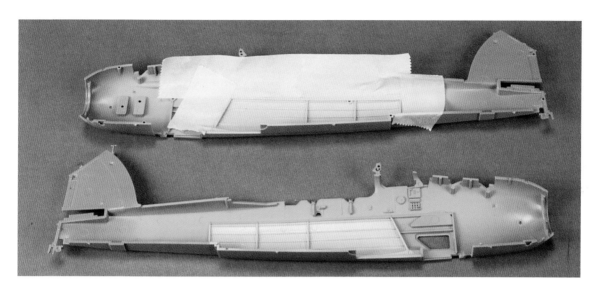

Fig. 6.2 The fuselage interior sides were sprayed Interior Green, then masked and sprayed with Gunze Light Sand.

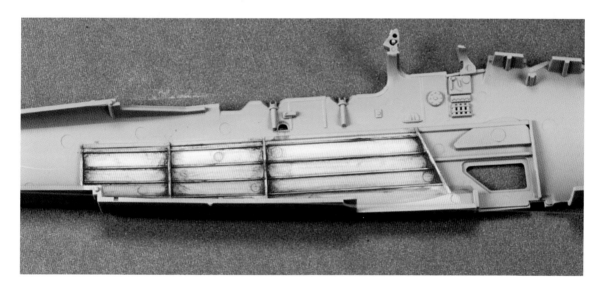

Fig. 6.3 The tan areas were given a 50/50 mix of Cadmium Red and Burnt Sienna oil paint to replicate worn red primer. Unfortunately, the injection pin marks were too obvious, so they were filled and sanded.

areas masked and sprayed with Gunze Sangyo Light Tan (Fig. 6.2). Cadmium Red and Burnt Sienna oil paints were combined in a 50/50 mix to achieve the red primer colour and applied over the tan fabric colour. It was at this point in the process that the realization dawned that the kit had numerous injector pin marks on the interior of the fuselage halves. These marks result from pneumatic pins pushing the moulded part from the mould during the manufacturing process. In most instances, these marks are well hidden and all but invisible, but on this kit it was decided that, invisible or not, they must be filled (Fig. 6.3). The oil paint was stripped, the holes puttied and sanded, and a coat of red primer paint applied, in lieu of the oils (Fig. 6.4).

The cockpit of the Swordfish is a kit in itself and requires very little in the way of additional details.

However, Eduard produces a small detail set for the model, which was used along with the proprietary Tamiya set (Fig. 6.5). The Eduard set features pre-painted, photo-etched seat belts and instru-

Fig. 6.4 The puttied area was painted with red primer, the sidewall fittings painted in flat black, and photo-etched parts attached.

Fig. 6.5 Tamiya's photo-etch set for the Swordfish includes the star-shaped engine cowl framework and bracing wires. This set is sold separately from the kit.

ment panel, just enough to provide that extra level of detail (Fig. 6.6).

The interior of the cockpit was painted and assembled according to the instructions, using RAF Interior Green, Alclad Aluminium and Testor's Metallizer Exhaust in lieu of flat black. While the Interior Green and Aluminium are self-explanatory, the use of Metallizer Exhaust might seem strange; however, the colour is in fact a dull black and, once dry, can be buffed to replicate worn metal, thus creating additional artificial contrast and highlights on the part.

The cockpit was given a wash of Blue-Black and the various Eduard photo-etched parts were installed before the cockpit framing was glued together (Fig. 6.7). The use of Blue-Black wash was deliberate – because of the open nature of the cockpit, more contrast was required. Although it appears too stark initially, once enclosed within the fuselage the results are quite satisfactory.

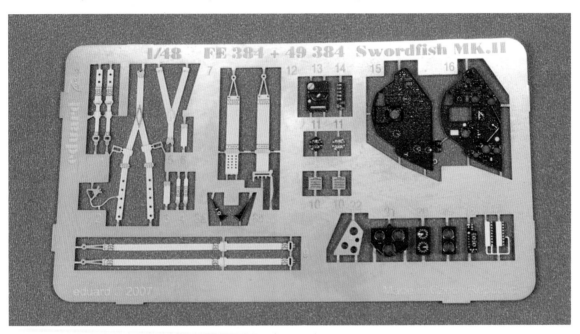

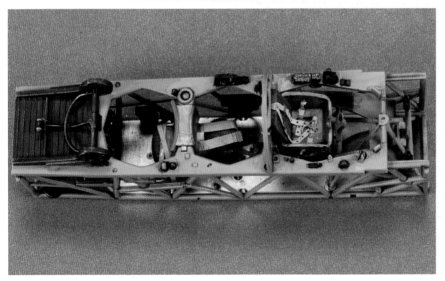

ABOVE: *Fig. 6.6 The Eduard 'Zoom' photo-etch set is a simplified version of the company's otherwise extensive detail sets. The Swordfish set includes the basics for the cockpit.*

Fig. 6.7 The finished cockpit frame ready for installation.

The kit's instrument panel was sanded and the photo-etched parts layered over the top (Fig. 6.8). The use of pre-painted parts was not widely accepted initially, as many felt that it defeated the purpose of actually building and painting. Over time, and as the quality of the parts has improved, the use of pre-painted instrument panels has provided modellers with a level of detail that few can achieve. Modellers will agree – the instrument panel is the most tedious part of the model, especially if that panel is visible in an open cockpit.

The two access windows on the fuselage sides were installed. Normally, clear parts are left until the final stages of construction, but with these two it's impossible to install them once the wings are on. The parts were installed and a generous layer of Micro Kristal Klear was applied to the exterior surfaces. Although any liquid masking material will work, Kristal Klear is effective (Fig. 6.9).

The cockpit assembly was test-fitted into the fuselage halves (Fig. 6.10) and, once satisfied that

Fig. 6.8 The photo-etched instrument panel fits perfectly over the kit part.

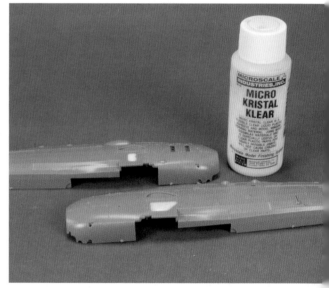

Fig. 6.9 The fuselage windows were installed and masked with Micro Kristal Klear, as it is impossible to install them once the fuselage is closed.

Fig. 6.10 The cockpit frame fits perfectly into the fuselage.

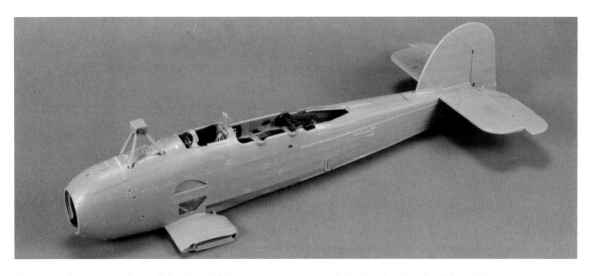

Fig. 6.11 The open cockpit of the Swordfish ensures that most of the interior detail will be visible.

Fig. 6.12 The engine cowling framework replaces the plastic arms of the kit part.

Fig. 6.13 The plastic arms were removed, the part painted and the metal part inserted in their place.

everything was in order, the halves were glued together and the remainder of the fuselage assembled according to the instructions (Fig. 6.11).

With the fuselage set aside, the decision was made to deviate from the instructions. By this point in the process, each model for this book had been a production line, focused on the construction and not really slowing down to enjoy the fun of the hobby. The kit instructions continued with the wings and, as previously mentioned, biplane wings are seldom easy. So it was decided to procrastinate on the wings, and actually 'finish' something far more appealing, the engine!

The 750hp Bristol Pegasus engine provided in the kit is very nicely moulded and Tamiya offers two photo-etched parts to detail the subframe for the engine cowling. The photo-etched parts from Tamiya were integrated into the engine assembly between the gearbox housing and the crankcase (Figs 6.12, 6.13), and are included in the kit instructions. The engine was sprayed with Testor's Metallizer Exhaust, buffed to a sheen, then given

a black wash around the cooling fins. Although the kit can certainly be built without the Tamiya detail set, which is sold separately, the extra detail it provides is readily apparent when the engine is assembled (Fig. 6.14).

The remaining parts were assembled and painted, including the engine's collector ring (Fig. 6.15). It has been a long-held contention that collector rings on Bristol-powered aircraft were a copper to bronze colour, much in the same way that anything with a Japanese Hinomaru was a Zero. Truth is, the collector rings were a nickel-steel alloy, which, when heated and cooled repeatedly, discoloured. The Swordfish's collector ring was sprayed with a 50/50 mix of Alclad Burnt Iron and Pale Burnt Iron at very low pressure, approximately 5psi, and the rest of the cowling painted white. At certain angles, the colour appears to have a bronze to copper hue, but in direct light the colour is far better matched to contemporary photos of both flying and non-flying historic aircraft. The engine was installed (Fig. 6.16) and provided the necessary emotional boost to get back to more serious matters – the wings.

Fig. 6.14 The metal parts add a level of detail that cannot be achieved with the plastic kit parts.

Fig. 6.15 The engine components ready for assembly.

Fig. 6.16 The engine components were a nice distraction, providing a sense of completion and motivation for the remainder of the project.

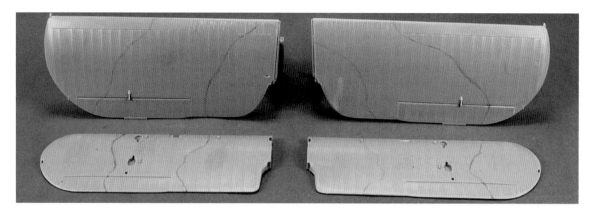

Fig. 6.17 The camouflage demarcations were pencilled directly on to the wings.

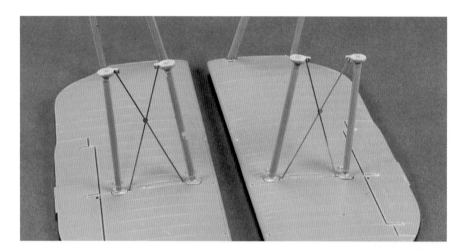

Fig. 6.18 Because of the construction process, combined with a logical painting process, the wing struts were attached to the upper wings prior to painting.

Fig. 6.19 The major subcomponents were painted using Tamiya White, Tamiya XF-63 for Extra Dark Sea Grey and Gunze Sangyo H422 RLM82 for Dark Slate Grey. These are not specific RAF labelled colours, but are very close matches based on research data.

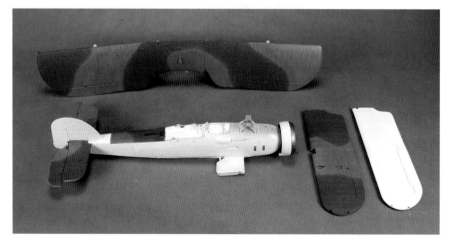

Assembly of the wings is a bit strange if one follows the instructions, as the model is engineered to have the wings either folded or extended. The builder must decide at this point in the process, as different wing struts are provided based on the wings' position. Using the kit instructions as a reference, the camouflage pattern for the wings was marked on to the parts (Fig. 6.17). The wing struts were glued to the underside of the upper wing and the photo-etched bracing wires installed (Fig. 6.18). The white was sprayed on the undersides using Tamiya Gloss White, and the camouflage colours of Tamiya XF-63 for the Extra Dark Sea Grey and Gunze Sangyo H422 RLM82 for Dark Slate Grey applied to the upper surfaces of the wings, fuselage and horizontal stabilizers (Fig. 6.19).

The windscreen was masked using 3M Kapton tape on both sides, sprayed flat black and attached to the fuselage. Again, conventional wisdom dictates that the clear parts should be applied last, but the windscreen is integral with the locator holes for the upper wing support struts. The instructions called for a flat black anti-glare panel, but some online research revealed that although flat black was a possibility, it was more likely that the camouflage colours carried on to the nose of the aircraft. Although the stark contrast of flat black would have been nice, the nose was masked and the camouflage colours carried on to the nose and engine cowling (Fig. 6.20).

After sitting for a few days curing, the model was given a wash of Ammo by Mig Blue-Black and wiped down. Swordfish were not particularly clean aircraft, so traces of the wash were left on the model to simulate grime and weathering (Fig. 6.21). The application of the wash at this point in the build is unusual, but experience dictates that once the wings are in place and the

Fig. 6.20 Although the kit instructions call for a flat black anti-glare panel, research determined that the camouflage colours were most likely carried on to the nose. The canopy was masked and installed at this point, as the structure is integral with the upper wing attachment points.

Fig. 6.21 Ammo by Mig provided the Blue-Black wash that was applied to the model.

Fig. 6.22 The photo-etched bracing wires were added to the model, starting with the innermost wires and working outwards towards the wingtips.

Fig. 6.23 The landing gear and radiator were installed. The engine pod was removed to facilitate assembly.

bracing wires installed, it is much easier to deal with sooner rather than later.

The wings were installed, the alignment checked, and the upper and lower struts set into place with Tamiya Extra Thin Cement. Although the struts align the wings quite well, care should be taken to ensure that the upper wing, despite its slightly swept-back nature, is symmetrically aligned with the lower wing. Although it might not seem to be critical, if the wings are not properly aligned, the pre-cut bracing wires will not fit.

After the wings dried, each of the stainless-steel photo-etched bracing wires were cut from the fret and attached to the model using cyanoacrylate glue. When working with biplanes and rigging,

an old adage from the sailing ship modellers holds true – always work from the inside out. Each of the innermost bracing wires are attached first, on both sides of the aircraft, working outwards towards the wingtips. This minimizes the risk of damaging wires already in place (Fig. 6.22).

With all of the bracing wires glued into place, it was time to attach the landing gear struts to the model (Fig. 6.23). This serves two purposes – it allows the model to sit under its own weight and makes it possible for the builder to adjust the height of the gear to ensure that the wings are equidistant from the ground. When the model was set down on its gear for the first time, one of the bracing wires became slack and bowed, a relatively common occurrence when using stainless-steel parts. The wire was broken loose from its connection point and reattached. In most instances, modellers can use monofilament for rigging lines, but in the case of the Swordfish, the wires are airfoil shaped.

With the wings and landing gear attached, the model was set aside to allow the countless attachment points to cure fully. Contrary to popular belief, CA glue, especially when used with CA accelerator, dries very quickly but takes a few hours to harden fully, something that should be kept in mind when using it to fill seams … sand them immediately!

With the model set aside, it was time for the small parts. Despite the complexity of this model, there are only a few, including the machine gun, Yagi radar arrays, prop, underwing racks and rails, and exhaust. As a modeller, one must come to terms with the inevitability of losing a part. Generally, it's not some obscure invisible part nestled deep in the fuselage, but, rather, some-

thing glaring, obvious and quite noticeable if left off. Such was the case with the Yagi radar array, located on each of the outboard wing struts (Fig. 6.24). There was one on the sprue, but the other – lost to the ages. The new modeller might fret, contact the company for a replacement, or simply leave the part off the model, but the experienced modeller looks at the part, breaks it down into its most basic shapes and builds a new one.

The part consists of: three dipoles, replicated with brass wire; the mounting rail, replicated with a square styrene stock; and the mounting clip, cut from a cross-section of plastic tube (Fig. 6.25). Using a no.75 drill bit in a pin vice, the holes were marked and drilled. Each of the sections of brass wire was sanded to square the ends and the cross-section of tube was cut into a C-shaped piece and glued to the frame. In the end, the scratch-built part was better scaled and more believable than the original kit part, so a second was built (Fig. 6.26). A small piece of modelling wisdom; if you can replace it with brass wire, it will almost always

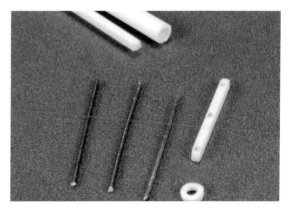

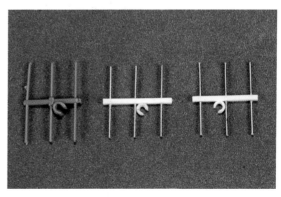

CLOCKWISE FROM ABOVE:

Fig. 6.24 The sole surviving Yagi array from the kit. The whereabouts of its counterpart are currently unknown.

Fig. 6.25 The basic components needed to scratch-build a new array – brass wire, square plastic stock and a cross-section of styrene tubing.

Fig. 6.26 The orphaned Yagi and the two replacements. The loss of a part like this is not a major issue – simply break the part down into its most basic shapes and scratch-build.

look better than its plastic predecessor. This is especially true with radar dipoles, pitot tubes, antennae and gun barrels.

The next step in the process was dealing with the porcupine exhaust, so-called because of the exhaust baffles. The kit part is moulded as a multi-piece assembly and each of the baffles is closed. Although there are several lovely aftermarket renderings available to replace this part, the kit part was assembled and each baffle opened using a dental probe (Fig. 6.27). The results were quite nice, with only a minor puncture wound to the hand, and the part was sanded smooth and painted with the same 50/50 mix of Alclad Burnt Iron and Pale Burnt Iron.

A modeller has the right, at any point in the process, to invoke artistic licence. Although the Swordfish was a superlative anti-submarine platform, it started life, and is most recognizable, as a torpedo plane. A study of 816 Squadron aircraft failed to show any aircraft operating from HMS *Tracker* in 1943 and carrying a torpedo. Photos

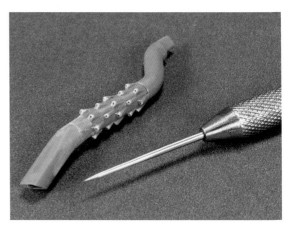

Fig. 6.27 The porcupine exhaust from the kit was detailed by opening each of the tabs with a steel probe. The results speak for themselves!

do show, however, that the centre-line rack was still in place, most likely for the carrying of depth charges. Is it possible that 816 Squadron aircraft *never* carried torpedoes in 1943? Certainly, and probably highly likely, as the role of the aircraft had changed and there was nothing left for Swordfish

Fig. 6.28 All of the major sub-assemblies, including the wing racks, are ready to go. Leaving these parts off the model while decaling prevents unnecessary breakage.

to attack with torpedoes. Is it possible that 816 Squadron aircraft could have carried torpedoes in 1943? Certainly, on a training mission perhaps. There is photographic evidence of Swordfish from other squadrons carrying a torpedo while equipped with wing racks and rocket rails, but the racks are always empty if a torpedo was carried. Regardless, a Swordfish looks out of sorts without a torpedo, so the torpedo rack was assembled, painted and attached to the underside of the model. With that, the sub-assemblies of the model were ready for attachment (Fig. 6.28).

The decals on this model are minimal, but they do add a level of colour to the model that really brings out the contrast of the white fuselage and camouflaged wings. The decals were applied with Micro Sol, allowed to dry, then sprayed with Vallejo clear flat. Once the clear dried and the model was able to be handled, the control horns for the rudder and elevators were drilled and 2lb monofilament was looped through a small piece of stainless-steel surgical tubing, each cut to length with a razor saw

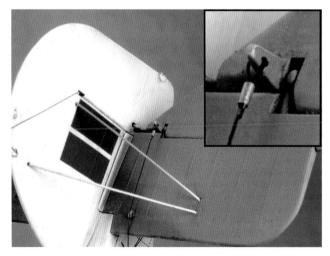

Fig. 6.29 Each of the monofilament control cables was looped through the pre-drilled control horns and threaded through a tiny piece of aluminum tubing.

(Fig. 6.29). This effectively replicates the way that the control cables were attached to the control surfaces. Each line was then fed through the appropriate opening in the fuselage, snaked through the cockpit, pulled tight (Fig. 6.29) and glued into place (Fig. 6.30).

The torpedo was assembled, painted with Testor's Metallizer Exhaust, polished to a sheen and installed. The antenna wire was glued into place at the tail using 2lb monofilament and CA glue, stretched, then attached to the mast on the upper wing. As the final step, the Kapton tape masks were removed from the windscreen and the model was complete (Fig. 6.31).

The Swordfish is an extremely well-engineered Tamiya offering that has withstood the test of time. Although a sturdy aircraft in real life, the model is fragile and careful handling is required. The wing alignment and bracing wires make this an intermediate-level kit. A total of sixty hours was spent on this model: twelve hours on the cockpit; forty hours on construction and rigging; and eight hours of painting and weathering.

The Swordfish is legendary, not for its stunning good looks and graceful lines, but because of its stability as a weapons' platform, its versatility and, most noticeably, its combat record. When the Swordfish is mentioned, with it goes

Fig. 6.30 The control cables were fed into the fuselage, pulled up through the cockpit for tension, then glued into place.

the attack on the French Fleet at Oran, the Italian Fleet at Taranto, the crippling of the German battleship *Bismarck*, and the destruction of more tonnage of Axis shipping than any other Allied aircraft. Although obsolete by 1939, it remained in service in front-line units until VE-Day, and formed the backbone of the Fleet Air Arm's anti-submarine force.

Fig. 6.31 The model was an easy build but requires patience, as the construction process is unorthodox for a typical aircraft model.

Fig. 6.32 Swordfish Mk II HS158 from 816 Squadron, the aircraft depicted by the
model, lands aboard HMS Tracker in 1943. FLEET AIR ARM ARCHIVES

Fig. 6.33 Deck hands
fold the wings of
HS158 in preparation
for her being struck
below deck. FLEET AIR
ARM ARCHIVES

Fig. 6.34 Swordfish LS326 is a beautifully restored aircraft operated by the Royal Navy Historic Flight. LA KEITH MORGAN/MOD PHOTO

Fig. 6.35 Modellers take note! Bristol rings are not painted bronze, but are various shades of discoloured nickel-steel alloy. VIC SCHEUERMAN

Fig. 6.36 LS326 with her wings folded back, offering a unique perspective of the aircraft. ALAN WILSON

Fig. 6.37 Swordfish Mk III HS554, on display at EAA's Airventure in Oshkosh, Wisconsin.
The aircraft is operated by Vintage Wings of Canada. JEFF BARRETTE

Fig. 6.38 Although air shows don't always afford the opportunity for great photos, even a photo in a crowd
can provide information that a modeller can use. This photo of HS554 provided a wealth of information in the
construction of the model. JEFF BARRETTE

Chapter Seven

Lancaster B III,
1/72 scale Hasegawa

AVRO LANCASTER, 57 SQUADRON, SEPTEMBER 1944
HASEGAWA 1/72 SCALE

Once in a while, you build a model for a specific reason, only to learn something about the actual aircraft or crew that changes your entire motivation. Such is the case of Lancaster LM624, DX-A 'A for Apple'. Initially, this aircraft was chosen simply because it carried a red tail fin, offering a splash of colour to what is, admittedly, a paint scheme carried by nearly all wartime Lancasters in Bomber Command. In researching the aircraft, a detailed history emerged of the aircraft and its subsequent disappearance and loss of her crew. The splash of colour no longer mattered, as it was now taken to a personal level, a human level.

The Hasegawa offering of the Avro Lancaster, 57 Squadron, September 1944 in 1/72 scale came as both a welcome relief and a let-down to Bomber Command modellers (Fig. 7.1). For decades, the only offerings in 1/72 were releases by Airfix, Matchbox and Revell in the 1960s; all

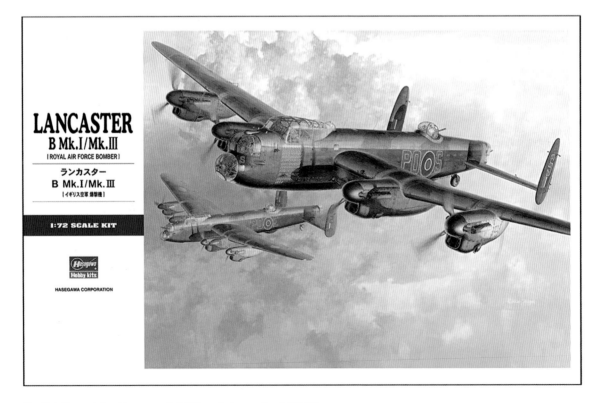

Fig. 7.1 Box art for Hasegawa's 1/72 scale Lancaster B I/III kit.

suffered accuracy issues and lack of detail. When Hasegawa released its kit in mid-2005, reviews were positive, save for the complaints about the lack of interior detail. Like the Mosquito, the canopy covers an already cramped cockpit, so lack of detail really wasn't a major concern.

The kit assembles well and the instructions call for an all-black interior. Fortunately, photos of 'S for Sugar', perhaps the most famous Lancaster of all time, clearly show a combination of both

Interior Green and black. The fuselage and cockpit floor, already sprayed black, received a light coat of Interior Green, effectively breaking up the monotone nature of the colours and providing some contrast, although admittedly this cannot be seen once the fuselage halves are closed (Fig. 7.2). Despite this, details within the cockpit were highlighted with a simple no.2 pencil to create a sheen along the edges of the details (Fig. 7.3). The pilot's seat received a rudimentary set of painted-

Fig. 7.2 Be wary of painting instructions. The kit called for an all-black interior, but research determined that this was not correct. Interior Green was applied in light coats over the black to replicate contrast. This is known as pre-shading.

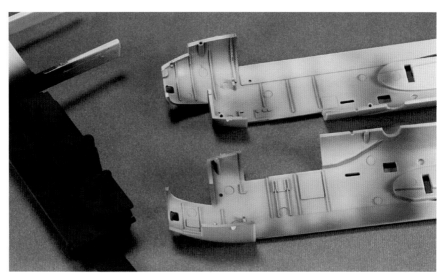

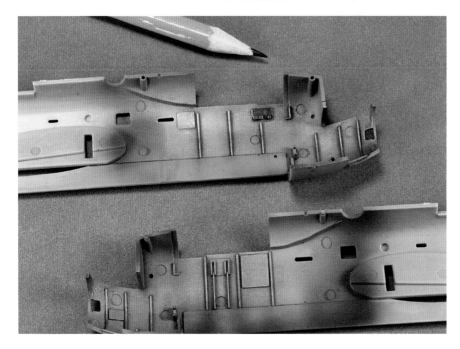

Fig. 7.3 A no.2 pencil was used to highlight edges of the details on the sidewalls.

on seat belts (Fig. 7.4) and the fuselage halves were unceremoniously closed up (Fig. 7.5).

Although it seems almost negligent for a modeller to put forth a half-effort like this, once the fuselage was closed it was nearly impossible to make out any details within the cockpit. With the canopy test-fitted on to the model, visibility into the cockpit was reduced even further, so it was decided to press on and focus on the exterior of the model. If, however, you choose to super-detail your Lancaster cockpit, Eduard produces an absolutely stunning photo-etched detail set for this specific kit (Fig. 7.6).

The fuselage halves were joined using generic MEK and a Touch-n-Flow applicator, manufactured by the Canadian firm Flex-I-File. The Touch-n-Flow

Fig. 7.4 After test-fitting the interior in the fuselage, it was determined that very little of the cockpit can be seen. As a result, not a lot of detail was added to the interior of the model. The seat belts were simply painted on to the pilot's seat.

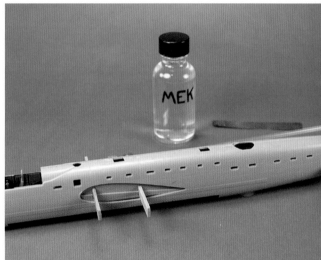

Fig. 7.5 The fuselage was closed up in relatively quick order using MEK.

Fig. 7.6 If the purist in you cannot deal with the lack of detail in the cockpit, have no fear, for Eduard does a spectacular interior detail set specifically for this kit. EDUARD

is essentially a capillary action surgical syringe, allowing minute amounts of MEK to be applied with a minimal amount of fuss.

A useful tool for joining long seams is an automotive spark-plug gap gauge. The very thin gauges are removed from the fan deck and work very nicely as glue shims (Fig. 7.7). Simply slip the shim between the parts, apply the liquid cement directly to the metal and allow capillary action to take hold (Fig. 7.8). For shorter runs, a single-edged razor blade works quite effectively (Fig. 7.9). Remove the shim, press the parts together

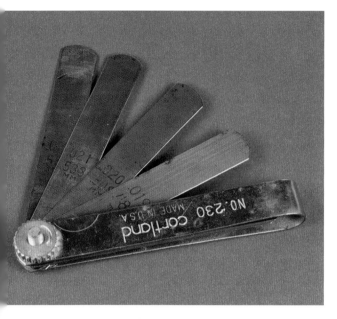

Fig. 7.7 An automotive spark-plug gap gauge, available in most auto shops, offers a nice assortment of thin, flexible metal shims. These work perfectly in seams when applying MEK liquid cement.

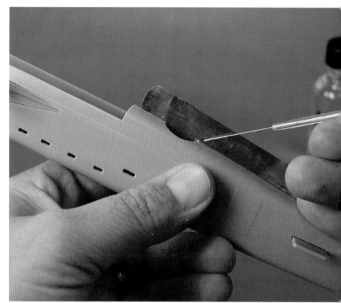

Fig. 7.8 Close the fuselage halves together with the metal shim between the two parts and apply the cement to the metal, not the plastic.

Fig. 7.9 A single-edged razor blade works well for shorter runs. Apply the cement to the metal and allow capillary action to work.

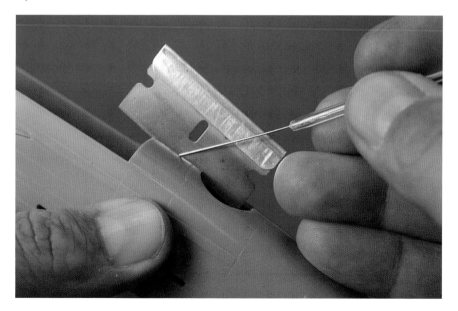

for fifteen to twenty seconds and the resulting join leaves a minimal amount of work to address (Fig. 7.10).

After the fuselage halves were joined, the seams were puttied using Tamiya Basic Modelling Putty and an artist's palette knife (Fig. 7.11). The

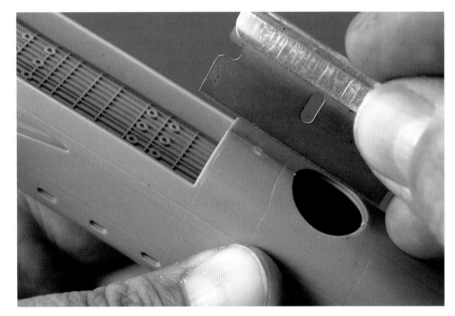

Fig. 7.10 When the cement has worked into the seam, remove the shim and squeeze the parts together for fifteen to twenty seconds.

Fig. 7.11 The model was puttied up using Tamiya Basic Putty and an artist's palette knife.

resulting seams were wet-sanded and inspected (Fig. 7.12). Seam issues along a wing or fuselage can often be hard to detect, but a simple trick to finding those issues involves a simple Sharpie permanent marker (Fig. 7.13). Simply colour the seam (Fig. 7.14), then sand with 600-grit paper. Any marker left in the recesses of the seam will

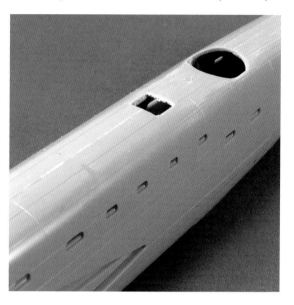

Fig. 7.13 A Sharpie-brand permanent marker offers a quick way to check seams.

Fig. 7.12 Looks can be deceiving – the seam is sanded, but it is difficult to tell if the seam will be invisible once painted.

Fig. 7.14 Simply scribble the seam with the marker and allow it to dry for a minute or two …

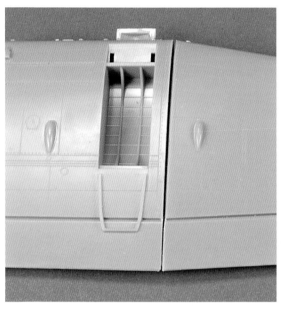

Fig. 7.17 The wings were scribed to a cut along the panel line on the underside of the wing, just outboard of the nacelle. The control surfaces were cut and the leading edge of the wing sanded to allow the dihedral to be reduced. The cuts were uniform on both wings, so that the angles would be the same on each side.

Fig. 7.15 … then wet-sand the seam; any residual marks left in the plastic will show up.

Fig. 7.16 The wings of the Lancaster are supposed to have 7 degrees of dihedral. The kit appears to have between 10 and 12 degrees, and simply does not look right.

show up, indicating that putty must be reapplied to the area (Fig. 7.15).

After the fuselage seams were addressed, the wings were attached and, immediately, something did not look right. The wings of a Lancaster carry 7 degrees of dihedral, which is quite noticeable in flight, but considerably less so when sitting on the ground. References showed a wide array of dihedral angles, ranging from 5 degrees to 12 degrees on some drawings. This is another instance of artistic licence taking hold and the decision was made to reduce the dihedral of the wings (Fig. 7.16). A cut was made on the underside of each wing, extended through the leading edge (Fig. 7.17). The cut was made using a scribing tool and each wing was cut at the same time to ensure that the width of the cuts was uniform. The leading and trailing edges were sanded to allow the wings to be flexed downward, reducing the dihedral. The underside cuts were closed using CA glue and accelerator, sanded smooth and the wings reinstalled on the fuselage, more closely matching the unloaded dihedral seen on the ground (Fig. 7.18). Although initially invoked under artistic licence, a photo emerged online of a Lancaster taken head-on and, sure enough, it appears that the modifications were, in fact, justified (Fig. 7.19).

Fig. 7.18 The dihedral looked much better once the wings were glued into place.

Fig. 7.19 Research comes through again. A straight-on photo of a Lancaster reveals that the new wing dihedral is much closer to the original than the kit originally was. RONNIE MACDONALD

Unfortunately, adjusting the dihedral of the wings caused the outboard engine nacelles to be out of alignment, as the engines are intended to hang vertical to the ground. While conventional wisdom would require either the cutting of one side or the shimming of the other to bring the nacelles back to their proper angle, each would have a negative impact on the joining of the nacelle to the wing. It was therefore decided that the outboard part of the nacelle would be sanded down, while the inboard side would be shimmed

with styrene, effectively 'splitting the distance' and bringing the nacelle back to vertical. The modification was simple and easy to make, and the nacelles were attached to the wing without difficulty (Fig. 7.20). The attachment points for the outside nacelles were filled with CA, polished and primed, and panel line detail was restored (Fig. 7.21). The resulting fix to the wings and nacelle brings the model closer to line drawings and photographs of actual aircraft.

Fig. 7.20 A simple fix isn't always without problems. Reducing the dihedral of the wings canted the outboard engine nacelles. Each nacelle was shimmed inboard and shaved down outboard, bringing them back to vertical.

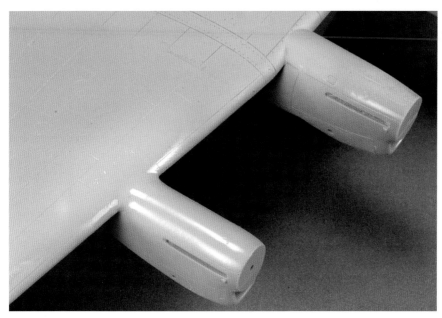

Fig. 7.21 The nacelles were filled and primed to check the contours. Panel lines were rescribed and rivet detail was added to the areas of the wing that were affected.

Fig. 7.22 The cockpit was packed with tissue and the entire model sprayed with Mr. Surfacer 1000 grey primer.

Fig. 7.23 The upper surface demarcation lines were masked and Gunze Sangyo Gloss Black was applied to the undersides of the model.

After checking all the seams, the cockpit area was packed with tissue and the model sprayed with Gunze Sangyo Mr. Surfacer 1000 (Fig. 7.22). The model was wiped down with a paper towel, the standard procedure for removing any residual powdered primer from the model, and the demarcation line between the upper surface camouflage colours and the black undersides and fuselage sides were masked. The model was sprayed with a coat of Gunze Sangyo Gloss Black and allowed to dry overnight (Fig. 7.23). The next day, the masks were removed from the upper surfaces and masks applied to the lower surfaces to protect the black-painted areas from overspray (Fig. 7.24).

The model was sprayed with several light coats of Gunze Sangyo Dark Green and Dark Earth, using a 'scribble pattern' of short strokes of light paint. This technique replicates the imperfect nature of paint application and gives the model very subtle tonal differences (Fig. 7.25). The masks were removed from the tail fins and a single vertical masking tape stripe applied to each fin. Masking tape was applied to the interior sides of the fins and the exterior was sprayed with Tamiya Gloss

Fig. 7.24 After the black paint had a chance to cure, it was masked off.

Fig. 7.25 The camouflage colours were applied in light coats in a scribble pattern, replicating the way that a 1/72 painter would spray the model. This adds some variety to the paint.

Red. The red paint was allowed to dry overnight with the rest of the model, and a few hours later the masks were removed to reveal a lovely red tail (Fig. 7.26).

This Lancaster was originally intended to be built as 'S for Sugar', perhaps the most famous Lancaster of all time and the current centerpiece at the Bomber Command Museum in Hendon, UK. Prior to the start of the build, it was decided that although 'S for Sugar' was perhaps the most logical choice, an aircraft with a splash of colour would be a nice diversion. An online search revealed an aftermarket decal sheet done by AeroMaster; the first in a series entitled 'Lancaster Bombers at War' and developed specifically for this kit. One of the

aircraft depicted in this sheet, LM624, carried the Squadron Leader's red tail (Fig. 7.27), that simple bit of colour that makes a model unique.

At this point in the process, the landing gear was assembled and fitted to the model (Fig. 7.28). This prevents the model from resting on its belly and minimizes the risk of damage to the underside paint.

The model was sprayed with clear gloss on the areas that were to receive decals. The fuselage sides were already Gloss Black, so no clear gloss was applied to the fuselage sides. Decals require patience, a gentle hand and a keen eye (Fig. 7.29).

Tools required for decals are few, but are critical; a pair of fine tweezers, a sharp no.11 blade,

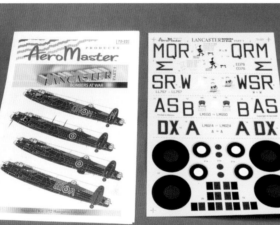

CLOCKWISE FROM TOP LEFT:

Fig. 7.26 The tail was striped and painted red. It had been decided earlier that this specific aircraft would be modelled simply because of the added colour.

Fig. 7.27 AeroMaster Decals offers a variety of markings specifically for this kit. The model chosen was a 57 Squadron aircraft, LM624.

Fig. 7.28 The landing gear struts were installed to minimize damage to the underside paint during decaling and final assembly.

Fig. 7.29 All set to decal the model. The wings received a coat of clear gloss to improve decal adhesion.

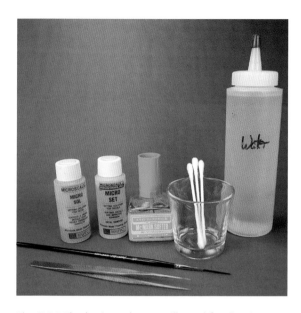

Fig. 7.30 The basic tools you will need for decaling your model.

Fig. 7.31 Carefully cut each decal as you apply it, as you only get one opportunity in most instances.

Fig. 7.32 Dip the decal in warm water mixed with a few drops of PVA. Allow it to soak in the water for thirty seconds.

Fig. 7.33 When the decal is removed, it will be curled. This indicates that the decal has not separated from the paper backing.

a clean, long-bristle brush, cotton buds and your favourite decal setting solution (Fig. 7.30). A piece of glass or acrylic is also handy as a work space if you have one available. Each decal is cut from the sheet using either a no.11 blade, or a pair of scissors (Fig. 7.31). Carefully cut close to the edges, leaving enough space for the decal to be handled, and dip each decal, one at a time, into warm water mixed with a few drops of PVA (Fig. 7.32). After a minute or two, the paper will become saturated and the decal will curl, so remove the decal from the water and lay it flat on the glass surface (Fig. 7.33). After

a few minutes the decal will flatten out (Fig. 7.34), and, with your clean paintbrush, move it slightly on the decal paper. If the decal moves freely, it is ready for application; if not, allow it to sit for a few more minutes. If the decal refuses to cooperate, soak it in water and allow the water to continue softening the layer of water-soluble glue holding the decal to the carrier paper.

Once the decal is moving freely on the carrier paper, apply decal setting solution to the surface of the model using a clean brush. A brush is preferred over a cotton bud so as to prevent any fibres from becoming trapped between the model's surface and the decal. Using tweezers to grip the

carrier paper, slide the decal on to the model using the brush to position it (Fig. 7.35). As long as there is setting solution or water between the decal and the model, it can be safely moved and positioned. After the decal is in position, use a cotton bud with a gentle rolling method to squeeze the water from underneath the decal, working from the centre of the decal outward (Fig. 7.36). As the decal begins to dry, you can apply more pressure to work it into panel lines and recesses. After fifteen minutes, apply more setting solution to the top of the decal to allow it to conform to the model. In most instances, decal setting solution is sufficient, but if the decals are having trouble

Fig. 7.34 When the decal has flattened out, gently moving it on the paper will tell you that it's ready to apply.

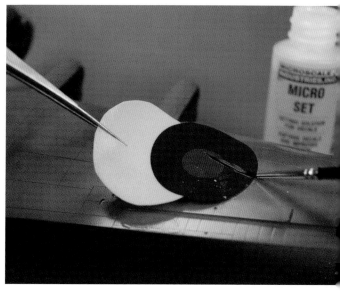

Fig. 7.35 Using tweezers to hold the paper and a clean, wet brush to move the decal, slide it on to the wing surface.

Fig. 7.36 Using a gentle touch and a cotton bud, work the water out from under the decal with a rolling motion. A dragging or wiping motion will move the decal.

Fig. 7.37 With the decals applied and set into place, the canopy, tail wheel and bomb-bay doors and tyres were added to the model.

Fig. 7.38 Each of the turrets was assembled and the framework painted with Vallejo Flat Black paint. When the lines got messy, a toothpick was used to clean them up.

conforming to the surface, decal solvent can be used. Solvent is simply a stronger, industrial-grade setting solution. Be warned, decals are extremely fragile during this process, as setting solutions will effectively melt the decal on to the model.

The model was set aside for several days to allow the setting solution to work, and during that time several applications of setting solution were made to the decals. Eventually, the model was sprayed with clear semi-gloss and the masked canopy glued into place, then the wheels and bomb-bay doors attached (Fig. 7.37).

The model was given an Ammo by Mig Dark Grey panel line wash on the upper surfaces and a Light Grey panel line wash on the undersurfaces, then wiped down. Because of the scale of

the model, weathering was kept to a minimum. The turrets of the model were assembled and the framework was hand-painted using Vallejo Flat Black and a thin liner brush. Although not as efficient as spraying, the use of Vallejo on the clear parts allows any inconsistent brush strokes to be cleaned up with a toothpick. Although the paint covers well, it does not bond to the clear plastic and is easily manipulated (Fig. 7.38).

Each of the turrets was installed, along with the four props and spinners and various antennae, and the model completed (Fig. 7.39).

Even with the wing dihedral issues and subsequent modifications, this was a quick and enjoyable build of only twenty-six hours, with equal amounts of time spent on construction and

Fig. 7.39 The model is now ready for the panel line wash and clear flat. The last step will be the antenna from the tips of the tails back to the canopy.

painting. Although the kit lacks a detailed interior, there are extensive interior sets in both resin and photo-etched brass available for this model should the builder choose to integrate them.

The following materials were used on this model:

- Gunze Sangyo H312 Kfir Green paint
- Gunze Sangyo H73 British Dark Green paint
- Gunze Sangyo H74 British Dark Earth paint
- Alclad Airframe Aluminium paint
- Alclad Burnt Iron paint
- Ammo by Mig – Light Grey Wash (undersides)
- Ammo by Mig – Deep Brown Wash (topsides)
- Ammo by Mig – Grey-Green Wash (interior)
- Gunze Sangyo H1 Black
- Warpigs Mid Rust pigment, Dark Earth pigment, Black pigment.

To many modellers, including details that are lost from view once the fuselage is closed is illogical and a waste of time and money, especially if aftermarket parts are being used. This decision is ultimately up to you, as it's your model, your time and your money. The decision to model 'A for Apple' instead of 'S for Sugar' adds to the satisfaction of knowing that, albeit inadvertently at the start, a connection was made not just to the machine, but also to the crew, and being able to research the names of the crew added a unique touch to the project.

Lancasters carried the brunt of Bomber Command's workload from 1942 until the end of the war. 'A for Apple' was a Lancaster III assigned to 57 Squadron, serial LM624, and carried codes DX*A. Research has turned up only a single, grainy photo of LM624, taken at East Kirkby. On the night of 6 September 1944, LM624 and her crew took off for a raid on the Dortmund-Ems and Mitterland canal system outside of Gravenhorst, Germany. The aircraft was posted as missing in action on 18 September. No trace of the aircraft or her crew was ever found.

Fig. 7.40 The dihedral of the Lancaster in flight more closely matches the kit. Perhaps the model should be built in flight? This is Lancaster RS689, a well photographed Lancaster B 1 from 50 Squadron, RAF. CANADIAN NATIONAL ARCHIVES

Fig. 7.41 A Lancaster control column fitted with dual controls for pilot training. The Lancaster flew with a single pilot. CANADIAN NATIONAL ARCHIVES

Fig. 7.42 The cockpit of perhaps the most famous Lancaster, 'S for Sugar', on display at the Bomber Command Museum. The cockpit of this aircraft is unrestored, giving the modeller a definitive source of information regarding colours. SHEB SHERBURN

Fig. 7.43 A fine study of the Lancaster's nose taken at the EAA Airventure, Oshkosh, Wisconsin, USA. This Lancaster is operated by the Canadian Warplane Heritage Museum and is the only Lancaster flying in North America, and one of two flying in the world. JEFF BARRETTE

Fig. 7.44 'Titus' displays fourteen successful missions while a crew member sits precariously on the nose in an obviously staged photo. A fall from that height would certainly hurt! Period photos such as this offer an excellent opportunity to compare and contrast details from contemporary aircraft appearing at airshows.
CANADIAN NATIONAL ARCHIVES

Fig. 7.45 The bomb-aimer's position in the nose of the Lancaster. The flat panel of Perspex was to prevent the distortion of the bomb-aimer's sight.

Fig. 7.46 The Battle of Britain Memorial Flight operates the only other airworthy Lancaster in the world. A lovely photo in its own right, to the modeller it offers a wealth of information, including the riveted texture of the fuselage and the contrast of the panel lines on the wings. SAC GRAHAM TAYLOR/MOD

Fig. 7.47 In 2015, the Canadian Warplane Heritage Museum repainted its Lancaster into the markings of KB732, 'Ex-Terminator', perhaps the most famous of Canadian Lancasters. The aircraft's original markings can be faintly seen behind the 'X'. JEFF BARRETTE

Fig. 7.48 The Lancaster's massive bomb bay. JEFF BARRETTE

Fig. 7.49 The tail turret of the Lancaster. Detailed photos such as this were rarely taken during wartime unless for technical purposes, so any opportunity to capture detail should not be passed on. JEFF BARRETTE

Fig. 7.50 PA474 heads down the runway, Merlins in perfect sync. The variations in the stressed-metal skin are obvious in this photo. RONNIE MACDONALD

Chapter Eight

Model Bases and the Art of the Diorama

Finishing a model, placing it on your shelf or in a cabinet, marks the end of the journey for that particular piece. For many, it marks the end of the project and time to move on to the next. For some, the time and effort expended on the project is not enough, and although the model is well built and well painted, it is still out of context sitting on a shelf (Fig. 8.1). There are several things that can be done to the model to enhance its visual appeal. The most simple is a base. Model bases are often more complex than the model themselves, but even a simple base can be effective at taking your model to the 'next level'.

Fig. 8.1 The ultimate goal of the diorama is to put life into the model. A simple backdrop and some Photoshop work, and it becomes reality.

Fig. 8.2 A simple trophy plaque and a pair of replica RAF pilots wings take the Hurricane from a 'model airplane' to 'museum model'.

Fig. 8.3 A plastic photo frame, some PVA glue and Woodland Scenics model railroad grass and you have an airfield.

The quickest and easiest model base is a simple trophy plaque. These pre-finished boards come in an endless variety of finishes and sizes and are available through your local trophy shop or online. Most trophy shops will happily do a small metal data plate for a reasonable fee, featuring the name of the aircraft and whatever pertinent information you feel is necessary. Sometimes utilizing a squadron insignia pin or a set of replica pilot's wings is enough to really set the model off (Fig. 8.2). For shows and model contests, models on bases inevitably enjoy more

attention, as the presentation of the model is superior to that of a model simply sitting on its registration form.

The next step in the process is a groundwork base. A groundwork base puts the model on a grass field, a dirt strip, or a carrier deck, adding to the historical and environmental context of the model. For most groundwork bases, a simple picture frame works well, providing a defined edge and a working space. Some white PVA glue and model railroad ground cover and you have a grass field (Fig. 8.3). Simply moving the model on

Fig. 8.4 The placement of a model on to a base immediately changes the overall appearance.

to the groundwork base drastically changes the visual appeal of the piece (Fig. 8.4).

Once you've acquired a photo frame sized to your model, remove the glass from the frame (set it aside and use it for your decaling), and use the wooden backing for the frame as your base (Fig. 8.5). The wooden backing is rough-sanded with 180-grit paper then marked with the squares to simulate the concrete slabs. The lines are scribed using a scribing tool and straight edge to create the illusion of individually poured concrete sections (Fig. 8.6). The lines are pre-shaded with black paint to create contrast (Fig. 8.7), then each of the squares is painted individually in random directions (Fig. 8.8). The triangular grass section in the corner of the base was scribed with random cuts and partially carved away, creating an uneven surface.

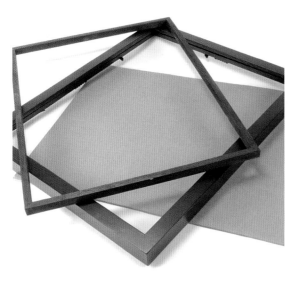

Fig. 8.5 A photo frame offers everything you need for a diorama base. Simply remove the glass.

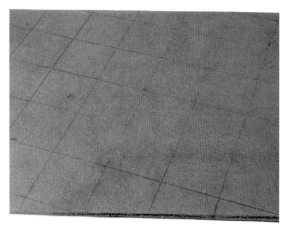

Fig. 8.6 The layout of the base was decided. To separate the angles of the base from the frame, the lines for the runway were drawn at a random angle then scribed into the particle board.

Fig. 8.7 The lines of the hardstand were sprayed with flat black paint, another instance of pre-shading.

Fig. 8.8 Each panel was painted with two different shades of grey, in a random pattern. This makes every concrete square look as if it was poured.

Most hobby shops have access to either pre-done groundwork available in sheets, or the Woodland Scenics brand of model-railway groundwork. Simply paint the area a dark brown colour, apply a thin layer of PVA glue, and spread the groundwork over the area. After thirty minutes, blow off the excess and you're ready to go (Fig. 8.9).

A simple coat of clear flat and the wooden base is reinstalled into the frame, and the project is complete (Fig. 8.10). The addition of the model on to the base immediately changes the entire visual dynamic of the project, taking it to the next level of presentation (Fig. 8.11).

The final step in the process is integrating your model into a diorama. A diorama is a snapshot

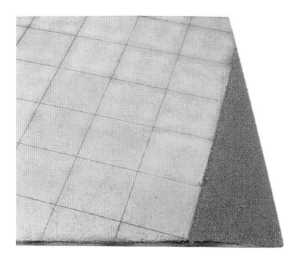

Fig. 8.9 The triangular corner of the base was carved out slightly with a heavy blade to create an uneven surface, then coated with PVA glue and Woodland Scenics model railroad groundwork.

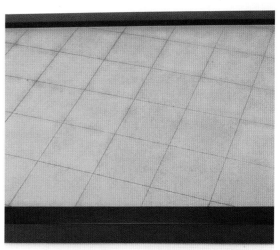

Fig. 8.10 The finished, albeit clean, hardstand is put back into the frame …

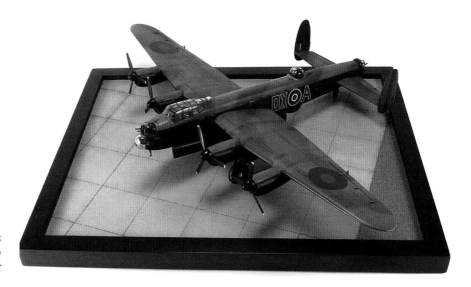

Fig. 8.11 … and gives the Lancaster an environmental context in which to sit.

of a moment in time, capturing not only your model, but everything else in its immediate environment, including people, vehicles and ancillary equipment. A diorama should convey a story of some sort, for example a boy on a bicycle staring longingly through a fence at a parked Spitfire, or a bomber crew preparing for its next mission.

With our simple groundwork base, we're going to take our 57 Squadron Lancaster and put it into a diorama. With the aircraft and the base complete, it was time to put the final touches to creating an environment for the model. This comes from Airfix and its lovely 1/72 RAF Bomber Command Re-Supply set (Fig. 8.12). The set contains nearly

Fig. 8.12 The Airfix RAF Bomber Re-Supply set is an absolutely perfect addition to the project. While the base itself lends environmental context, vehicles and figures add life and activity to the setting, taking it from a simple model on a base to a fully fledged diorama.

Fig. 8.13 Czech Master Kits, or CMK, does an extensive line of 1/72 resin figures. Although this set is designed specifically for the Wellington, it can work for any RAF aircraft.

Fig. 8.14 CMK's RAF Pilots Before Flight does a perfect job of conveying that age-old military policy of 'Hurry up and wait'

everything needed to get your Lancaster ready for its next mission. The human element of the diorama is provided by CMK from the Czech Republic, in the form of three RAF ground-crew (Fig. 8.13), and three RAF aircrew figures, cast in resin (Fig. 8.14). The figures are cast with separate limbs and must be assembled using CA (Fig. 8.15). After assem-

bly, the figures are primed and ready for paint (Fig. 8.16). Fortunately, painting figures in 1/72 scale does not require huge amounts of artistic talent, so the uniforms and flying gear were painted with various shades of brown and blue and the faces painted with Vallejo Flesh Base. The figures were given a brown wash and sprayed with clear flat.

Fig. 8.15 Each figure requires assembly and with resin you have no choice but to use CA glue. Liquid cement doesn't affect resin. Each of the parts was cut carefully with a razor saw. If you think 1/72 aircraft are small, try 1/72 figures!

Fig. 8.16 Each figure was assembled and primed, but left on its casting block so that it could be easily held during painting. The sitting figure is a nice pose, as it is unconventional.

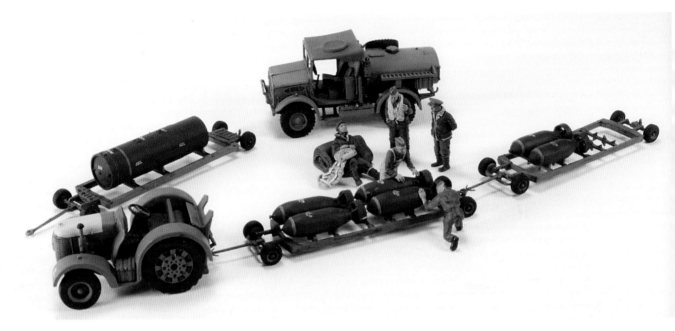

Fig. 8.17 The figures and vehicles were painted according to photos, weathered and sprayed with clear flat. An entire volume could be written simply on the painting of figures and vehicles.

Fig. 8.18 The positions of the figures and vehicles were determined by simply moving them about on the base and deciding what provided an acceptable balance.

Fig. 8.19 The figures and vehicles were glued to the base, but the model was not. Instead, a set of wheel chocks was glued to the base, so that the model occupies the exact same spot on the base each time it's moved.

Simply because there are 400 pieces in the airfield set doesn't mean that we need to use everything. The key to a diorama is keeping it realistic and believable. Despite the frenzied activity at an airfield prior to a mission, everything on the field and around the aircraft had a purpose. All of the vehicles were built and painted at the same time, an evening's worth of work, and washes and weathering applied (Fig. 8.17).

The parts were arranged on the base using various historical photos as references and after four or five different layouts, the positions were selected and the vehicles and figures attached using small amounts of CA glue (Fig. 8.18). Although the figures and accessories were glued to the base, the aircraft model was not, allowing it to be packed separately for shows and displays.

Also, the base could be used for another project at a later time, perhaps a Halifax or a Wellington (Fig. 8.19).

In truth, the diorama serves multiple functions. First, it puts the model into environmental context and provides a human element to the model. A good diorama will 'set the stage' and tell a story. Second, it increases the visual appeal of the model. And finally, it provides a solid foundation for the model to sit on, reducing the chances of breakage from handling.

The Airfix diorama set, the figures and the creation of the base was a quick process, approximately twelve hours of work. It serves as a superb backdrop to the Lancaster and provides an element of realism beyond a simple wooden display base.

Chapter Nine

Royal Air Force Camouflage and Markings 1939–45

Volumes have been written on RAF camouflage during World War II. Each time a consensus is reached by historians regarding the standardization of paint and national markings, a photo surfaces showing some anomaly that flies in the face of standardization. Although the world's perception of RAF camouflage is the ubiquitous Dark Green and Dark Earth scheme, the variations of camouflage practices and national insignia prior to the outbreak of war are too numerous to mention in a few short paragraphs. Instead, we will focus on RAF camouflage and national insignia after September 1939.

Prior to 1940, aircraft camouflage schemes, colours and markings were under the auspices of the Directorate of Technical Development, which was transferred to the Air Ministry, along with the Production and Research Directorates, and merged into the Ministry of Aircraft Production. In 1941, six generic camouflage patterns were developed, each a general outline for factories and maintenance units. In addition, manufacturers prepared camouflage design sheets for specific aircraft to ensure some degree of consistency throughout production. To further confuse issues, drawings

A spectacular photo of the Battle of Britain Memorial Flight Spitfire and Hurricane in formation over the English countryside. This photo could easily have been taken in the summer of 1940. Both aircraft carry the standard 1940 Day Fighter scheme of Dark Earth and Dark Green over Sky. SAC NEIL CHAPMAN/MOD

Battle of Britain Memorial Flight Spitfire Mk Vb AB910 banks for the camera. This aircraft carries the standard Temperate Land Scheme of Dark Green and Ocean Grey over Medium Sea Grey with Sky ID band, Sky spinner and codes, and yellow leading-edge stripes. CPL NEIL CONDI RAF/MOD

were inconsistent, with pattern drawings from the Ministry of Aircraft Production Standards of orders of 1943 different to those that appear in Air Ministry Publication 2656A *External Colour of Aircraft*, 1944, and various Air Ministry orders appearing between 1942 and 1945.

SPITFIRE

In 1939, the Air Ministry's standard camouflage scheme for day fighters was Dark Earth and Dark Green in Type A or B camouflage schemes as dic-

tated by Air Ministry Publication 970. Aircraft with even numbered serials were supposed to receive Type A schemes, while odd-numbered serials were supposed to receive Type B schemes, which was a mirror opposite of Type A. However, in many instances, this was applied to the first aircraft of a production batch, regardless of the serial number. In fact, Supermarine's first production Spitfire, K9787, carried a Type A scheme, while the second, K9788, carried Type B, exactly opposite of that prescribed in the Air Ministry Publication! This practice was discontinued on 14 January 1941 and all aircraft manufactured after that date carried the Type A scheme only.

Spitfire underside camouflage during 1939 was a confused collection of various types of roundels, aluminium and night undersurfaces, aluminium and white with control surfaces in alternating colours, underwing roundels Type A, no underwing roundels and underwing roundels on one side. A modeller replicating an early war fighter should certainly reference photos of specific aircraft, as new orders were being applied to production aircraft at the factories, but were also being issued to units in the field, who may or may not have applied them in a timely fashion due to operational activity. This is especially noteworthy of the Battle of Britain period of 10 July to 31 October 1940.

By the start of war in September 1939, most squadrons had been repainted to the standardized practice of starboard side undersurfaces in white, portside undersurfaces in night (black), with no underside roundels. This scheme remained in effect until June 1940, when orders instructed the undersurfaces to be repainted in overall Sky with no roundels.

Type A roundels, 50in (1,270mm) in diameter, were officially introduced from 11 August 1940, although it took some time for Fighter Command to standardize its squadrons. In fact, most Fighter Command aircraft in operation continued to wear the split camouflage undersides until an Air Ministry order in April 1941 directed all aircraft to be painted Sky with Type A roundels. Spinners were changed to Sky, in addition to an 18in (457mm) Sky fuselage band, on all day fighters after 27 November 1940. By late 1940, confusion again reigned despite the Air Ministry orders, and aircraft appeared with an array of underside markings and colours.

By 1941, with the Battle of Britain over and the RAF receiving upgraded Mk V Spitfires, camouflage practices began to standardize as the Mk I and Mk II aircraft were relegated to second-line and training units. Spitfires arrived from factories with Dark Green and Dark Earth upper surfaces, Type B wing roundels, Type A.1 fuselage roundels, Sky undersurfaces with spinners and fuselage band, and Type A underwing roundels. This remained the standard Spitfire scheme until August 1941, when Dark Earth was replaced by Ocean Grey and Sky undersides were replaced with Medium Sea Grey. The Sky spinner and fuselage band was retained, although many aircraft had their spinners painted in either Ocean Grey or Medium Sea Grey.

Squadron codes prior to August 1941 had been officially mandated at 48in (1,219mm) in height, with 6in (152mm) stroke, but this large size had proved problematic on Spitfires due to the narrow fuselage. Squadrons were allowed to apply their codes using their own discretion, so variations were commonplace. After August 1941, Spitfire squadron codes were standardized at 24in (610mm), painted Sky.

In addition to the colour changes, a 4in (102mm) yellow strip was carried on the leading edges of day fighters to aid in 'friend or foe' recognition, as no German aircraft carried leading-edge markings. The length of markings outlined in drawings, however, varied according to field applications.

Spitfire markings did not change again until May 1942, when the Type A.1 fuselage roundels were replaced with Type C.1. This became the standard camouflage scheme for day-fighter Spitfires throughout the remainder of the war.

HURRICANE

If Spitfire camouflage practices were confused, then Hurricane practices were complete mayhem between early 1939 and May 1942. Although Hurricane camouflage schemes mirrored those of the Spitfire (as both fell into the category of single-engine day fighters), operational anomalies on Hurricanes were far more prevalent due to their earlier operational debut and subsequent numbers.

Hurricanes appeared operationally wearing Dark Green and Dark Earth upper surfaces, also utilizing the Type A and Type B camouflage schemes. Like the Spitfire, however, Hurricane schemes

Hurricane LF363 from the Battle of Britain Memorial Flight on touchdown. CPL PHIL MAJOR RAF/MOD

did not follow the mandate of even-numbered serials receiving Type A and odd-numbered serials receiving Type B schemes. In fact, the first production Hurricane carried serial L1547 and a Type A scheme. Modellers should refer to specific aircraft photos when determining what scheme to carry. The use of Type B schemes, like the Spitfire, was discontinued on 14 January 1941 and all subsequent Hurricanes produced after this date carried Type A schemes only.

Leading up to the Battle of Britain, Hurricanes usually wore the standard 'Night and White' scheme on their undersurfaces, with no underwing roundels. Orders dictated the use of all Sky undersides with no roundels on 6 June 1940. By the start of the Battle of Britain, the standard Hurricane scheme was *supposed* to consist of Dark Green/Dark Earth Type A or B scheme, 49in (1,245mm) diameter Type B upper wing roundels, 35in (890mm) diameter Type A.1 fuselage roundels, Sky undersurfaces with no wing roundels until after August 1940, after

which 50in (1,270mm) diameter Type A roundels were applied.

The RAF went back to the 'Night and White' scheme for a short period of time in November 1940; however, it was mandated that painting the port wing black over the Sky underside was acceptable. This also marked the implementation of the 18in (457mm) Sky fuselage band and Sky spinner. In the case of the underwing roundels on the port wing, a yellow ring was applied to the roundel to provide a demarcation between the blue outer ring of the roundel and the black underside.

The 'Night and White' scheme prevailed until 22 April 1941, when units were again ordered to repaint into Sky with Type A roundels. The reasoning for this is not known, but historians lean towards the RAF's role as a defensive force changing to that of an offensive force over the Continent.

Hurricane camouflage remained unchanged until August 1941, when, like the Spitfire, Dark

Earth was replaced with Ocean Grey and undersides replaced with Medium Sea Grey. The Sky spinner and fuselage bands were retained and squadron codes in grey were replaced with Sky. It was not until May 1942 that Hurricanes adopted the yellow leading-edge stripes and Type C.1 roundels. This became the standard camouflage scheme for Hurricane day fighters, although the Hurricane pressed on in the night fighter and fighter-bomber roles with a variety of schemes.

MOSQUITO

De Havilland's 'Wooden Wonder' is the epitome of the multi-role aircraft and, as a result, it carried a wide array of camouflage schemes during its operational tenure. For the sake of brevity, we'll focus on the Mosquito FB VI.

By the time the FB VI Mosquito was operational, the May 1942 changes to RAF camouflage had long been in effect. Mosquito FB VI aircraft initially appeared with the standard day-fighter scheme of Dark Green and Ocean Grey upper surfaces with 54in (1,372mm) diameter Type B wing roundels, 36in (914mm) diameter Type C.1 fuselage roundels and Medium Sea Grey undersurfaces with no roundels. Initially appearing with Sky spinners and an 18in (457mm) fuselage band, these were quickly painted out.

By June 1943, most FB VI Mosquitoes were appearing in night-fighter camouflage, consisting of Dark Green and Ocean Grey uppers, with Night undersurfaces. Spinners were usually painted in Medium Sea Grey.

Coastal Command Mosquitoes often appeared in overall Dark Sea Grey with Sky undersides. Once again, specific aircraft should be referenced by photos, as Mosquitoes wore a wide array of colour based on their specific roles, including overall Night, overall PRU Blue, natural metal and Dark Green/Dark Earth with Azure Blue.

Mosquito B IV DZ353 in formation with DZ367 sometime between 23 November 1942 and 30 January 1943. DZ367 was lost on 30 January over Berlin and DZ353 was lost over Rennes, France, on 8 June 1944. USAF

Swordfish LS326 over the English countryside, wearing Dark Slate Grey and Extra Dark Sea Grey over White, with Type C.1 fuselage roundels and Type B wing roundels. LA ABBIE HERRON/MOD

SWORDFISH

The 'Stringbag' wore a relatively common scheme during the war years with a few subtle variations. Upper surface colours were predominantly Extra Dark Slate Grey and Dark Sea Grey, initially over Sky, and, by 1943, White. Markings consisted of 56in (1,422mm) diameter Type B roundels on the upper wings, 36in (914mm) diameter Type C.1 roundels on the fuselage sides, and no underwing markings. In most instances, the underside colours rose as much as 50 per cent up the sides of the fuselage. By 1943, they rose to the edge of the upper fuselage curve when viewed from above.

Early on in the war, counter-shading was done by utilizing Dark Slate Grey for the top planes and Light Slate Grey for the bottom planes. Modellers will need to refer to aircraft photos to determine if shading was used on a specific aircraft.

LANCASTER

The Lancaster is one of the few RAF aircraft whose camouflage scheme didn't change during its operational career. Upper surface colours consisted of Dark Green and Dark Earth over Night. The undersurface colours extended 75 per cent up the side of the fuselage and engine nacelles. The vertical tail fins were also Night. Markings consisted of 96in (2,438mm) diameter Type B wing roundels, 54in (1,372mm) diameter Type C.1 fuselage roundels and 48in (1,219mm) high squadron codes.

Lancaster PA474 of the Battle of Britain Memorial Flight on flyby. RONNIE MACDONALD

RAF COLOURS – HOW CLOSE IS CLOSE?

There are many factors to consider when painting your model and, surprisingly, the accuracy of the colour is not at the top of the list. Although there are very accurate representations of the colours applied to wartime aircraft, several factors must be considered:

- Who manufactured the paint in 1942?
- Was the paint mixed properly at the factory?
- Was the paint stirred sufficiently by the painter at the aircraft factory?
- Was the paint applied over a dark or light surface by a mechanic at the field?
- How long was the paint on the aircraft?
- What degree of oxidation or fading has the paint experienced?

When one considers these simple questions, any of which can alter the shade of the paint being applied, it is easy to see that the perfect shade of paint for your model is a lesson in futility. To that end, we have included two useful resources, a cross-reference chart showing current paint manufacturers and the specific colours they offer, and a printed colour chart. The printed colour chart demonstrates the variations and interpretations of multiple sources of data – some are in agreement and others are not. All four columns of colour were replicated on a gamma-corrected monitor for consistency. The first is a scan of an original set of Air Ministry paint chips, the second is a 1956 set of Royal Air Force reproduction colour chips, the third column is a collection of current CMYK data, and the fourth column is simple RGB data plugged into Adobe Photoshop software. What all of these colour samples indicate is that although not perfect, all are very close.

Scale factor should also be a consideration. Scale factor is the intensity of the colour at the perceived distance relative to the size of the model. For example, the dark green of a real Spitfire will appear lighter as the distance between the viewer and the aircraft increases. Many modellers factor scale into their colours by lightening the paint so that a 1/48 scale model 1ft (305mm) away has the same colour saturation as a real aircraft 48ft (14,630mm) away.

World War Two Royal Air Force Colours

Scanned Originals	Scanned Reproduction	Digital Reproduction	Simple RGB
Scanned at high resolution from an original 1944 Air Ministry technical manual.	Scanned from a reproduction paint chip set of RAF and FAA colours printed in 1956.	Utilizing 1929 Munsell Book of Color Standards and digitally recreated to match hue, value, and chroma.	RGB values plugged into Adobe Photoshop.
Dark Green			
Dark Earth			
Ocean Grey			
Dark Slate Grey			
Dark Sea Grey			
Medium Sea Grey			
Extra Dark Sea Grey			
Middlestone			
PRU Blue			
Interior Grey Green			
ID/Trainer Yellow			
Dull Red			
Dull Blue			
Sky Grey			

The reproduction of these colours is intended as a guide, as printer's ink cannot accurately recreate these colours as originally formulated.

RAF COLOUR TABLE

Colour name	FS595	Mr. Paint	Humbrol	Life Color	Colour Coats	Tamiya	Xtracolor	Model Master	Revell	Gunze Sangyo	Vallejo Model Air	Ammo by Mig	AK Interactive
Dark Earth	FS33105	MRP108	30	UA092	ACRN10	XF-52	X:X2	2054	32182	H72	71.323	70	2012
Dark Green	FS34079	MRP110	29	UA091	ACRN09	XF-81	X:X110	2060	32139	H73/H309	71.324	915	2011
Sky/Type S/Duck Egg Blue	FS34583	MRP118	90	UA095	ACRN01	XF-21		2049	32159	H74	71.302	243	2015
Ocean Grey	FS36152	MRP115	106	UA093	ACRN07	XF-82	X:X6	2057		H335	71.273	245	2014
Medium Sea Grey	FS36270	MRP112	165	UA094	ACRN04	XF-83	X:X3	2058		H306	71.307	246	2013
Middle Stone*	FS33440	MRP121	225	UA097	ACRN11	1:1 XF-59 +XF-60	X:X9	2052	32116	H71	71.031		2016
Azure Blue	FS35231	MRP119	157	UA098	ACRN34	1:1 XF-18 +X-14	X:X26	2048			71.108		2017
Extra Dark Sea Grey	FS36118	MRP114	123	UA022	ACRN02	XF-63	X:X130	1723	32174	H333/H305	71.110		
Dark Slate Grey	FS34096	MRP117	224	UA054	ACRN06		X:X25	2027	32165		71.309		
PRU Blue	FS35164	MRP120	230	UA045	ACRN14		X:X008				71.109		
Dark Sea Grey	FS36173	MRP113	164	UA046	ACRN03	XF-54		2059	36177	H75/H331	71.405		
Night Black	FS37038	MRP137	21	LC02	ACRN17	XF-1		1749		H452	71.057		
White	FS37778	MRP004	22	LC01	ACRN37	XF-2		1745					
Trainer/ID Yellow	FS33538	MRP122	24	UA140	ACRN21	XF-3	X:X11	2063		H329	71.078		
Interior Grey-Green	FS34226	MRP111	78	UA060	ACRN28	XF-71	X:X11	2062		H312	71.305	244	
Dull Blue	FS35044	MRP124	25	LC35	ACRN31			1719					
Dull Red	FS31136	MRP123	153		ACRN27			2009	32179				
Identification White	FS37875	MRP004	34	LC01	ACRN37	XF-2		1745		H316	71.279		
Aluminium	FS37178	MRP008	56	LC24		XF-16							

Hawker Hurricane Camouflage Scheme post May 1942

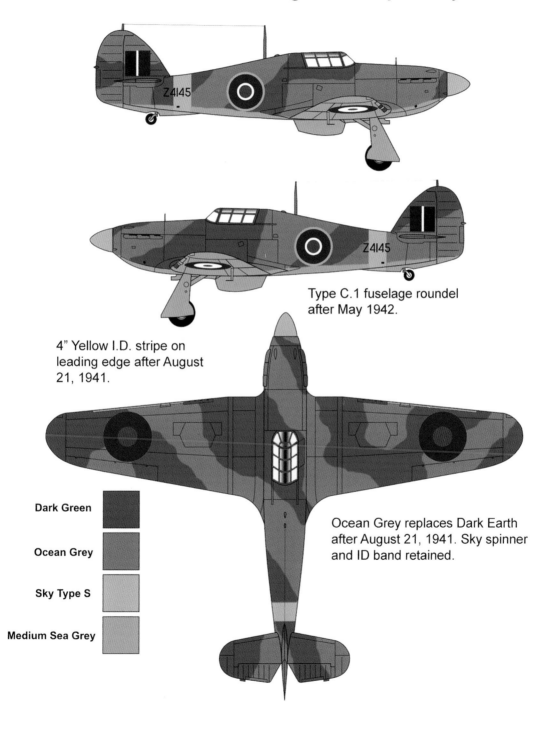

Type C.1 fuselage roundel after May 1942.

4" Yellow I.D. stripe on leading edge after August 21, 1941.

Dark Green

Ocean Grey

Sky Type S

Medium Sea Grey

Ocean Grey replaces Dark Earth after August 21, 1941. Sky spinner and ID band retained.

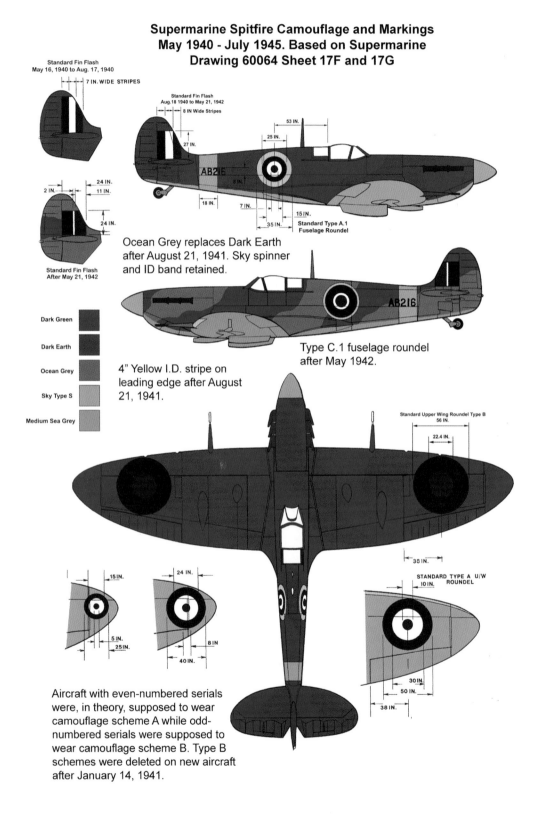

Supermarine Spitfire Camouflage and Markings May 1940 - July 1945. Based on Supermarine Drawing 60064 Sheet 17F and 17G

Standard Fin Flash
May 16, 1940 to Aug. 17, 1940

7 IN. WIDE STRIPES

Standard Fin Flash
Aug.18 1940 to May 21, 1942

8 IN Wide Stripes

27 IN.

53 IN.

25 IN.

AB216

24 IN.

11 IN.

2 IN.

24 IN.

8 IN.

18 IN.

7 IN.

15 IN.

35 IN.

Standard Type A.1
Fuselage Roundel

Standard Fin Flash
After May 21, 1942

Ocean Grey replaces Dark Earth after August 21, 1941. Sky spinner and ID band retained.

AB216

Dark Green

Dark Earth

Ocean Grey

Sky Type S

Medium Sea Grey

Type C.1 fuselage roundel after May 1942.

4" Yellow I.D. stripe on leading edge after August 21, 1941.

Standard Upper Wing Roundel Type B
56 IN.

22.4 IN.

38 IN.

STANDARD TYPE A U/W ROUNDEL
10 IN.

15 IN.

24 IN.

5 IN.

25 IN.

8 IN

40 IN.

30 IN.

50 IN.

38 IN.

Aircraft with even-numbered serials were, in theory, supposed to wear camouflage scheme A while odd-numbered serials were supposed to wear camouflage scheme B. Type B schemes were deleted on new aircraft after January 14, 1941.

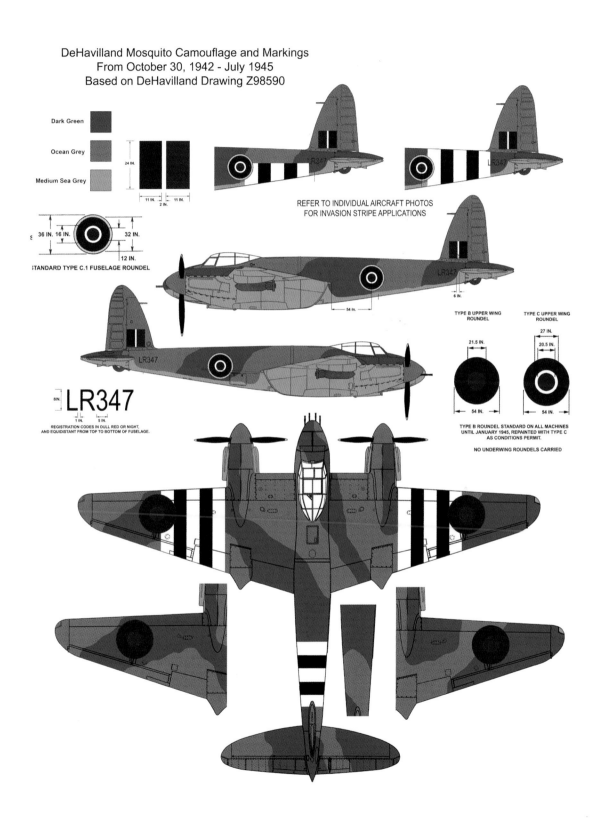

DeHavilland Mosquito Camouflage and Markings
From October 30, 1942 - July 1945
Based on DeHavilland Drawing Z98590

Dark Green

Ocean Grey

Medium Sea Grey

24 IN.

11 IN.   11 IN.
2 IN.

REFER TO INDIVIDUAL AIRCRAFT PHOTOS
FOR INVASION STRIPE APPLICATIONS

36 IN. 16 IN.   32 IN.

12 IN.

STANDARD TYPE C.1 FUSELAGE ROUNDEL

6 IN.

54 in.

LR347

8IN. LR347

1 IN.   5 IN.
REGISTRATION CODES IN DULL RED OR NIGHT,
AND EQUIDISTANT FROM TOP TO BOTTOM OF FUSELAGE.

TYPE B UPPER WING
ROUNDEL

TYPE C UPPER WING
ROUNDEL

27 IN.

21.5 IN.

20.5 IN.

54 IN.   54 IN.

TYPE B ROUNDEL STANDARD ON ALL MACHINES
UNTIL JANUARY 1945, REPAINTED WITH TYPE C
AS CONDITIONS PERMIT.

NO UNDERWING ROUNDELS CARRIED

Fairey Swordfish 1944 Camouflage Scheme

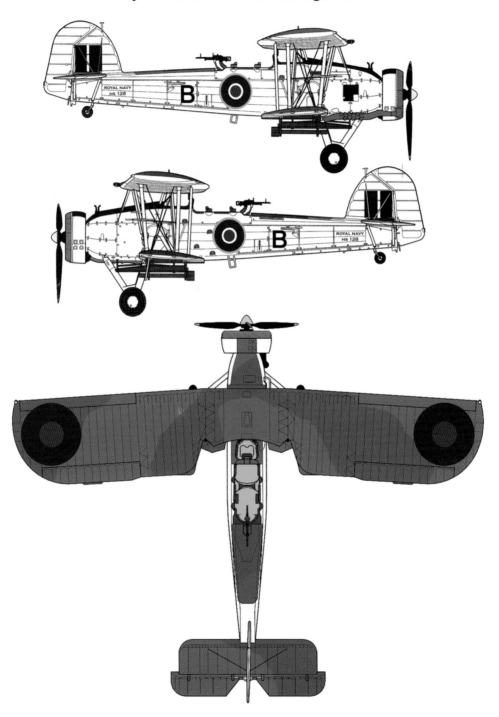

Avro Lancaster Typical Camouflage Scheme

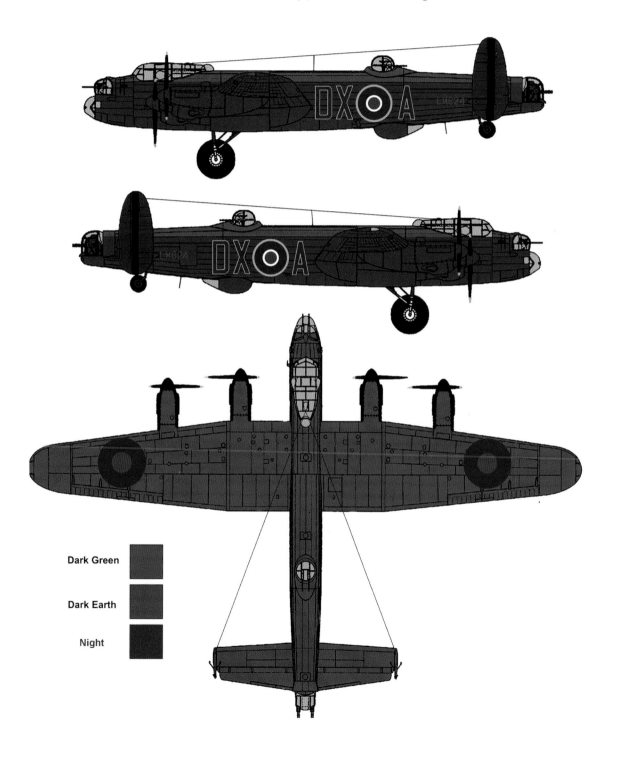

Dark Green

Dark Earth

Night

RAF/FAA National Insignia 1939-45

Type A Roundel. Used primarily on the undersides of aircraft from 1939 to 1942. Colors consisted of Dull Blue, White, and Dull Red in a 1:3:5 ratio. Standard underwing size was 50in for Spitfires and Hurricanes until replaced with Type C.1 in June 1942.

Type A.1 Roundel. Used on all camouflaged surfaces from 1937 to March of 1939, as fuselage roundels until July 1942. Colors consisted of ID Yellow, Dull Blue, White, and Dull Red in a 1:3:5:7 ratio. Replaced by Type C.1 roundel in July, 1942. Typically 35in for Spitfires and Hurricanes.

Type A.2 Roundel. Alternative to Type A.1 appearing on aircraft from 1940-1942. No orders exist for its prescription, and could simply be a misinterpretation of orders. Colors are the as Type A.1 in a ratio of 1:3:5:6.

Type B Roundel. Used as upper surface roundel on vast majority of RAF and FAA aircraft until 1947. Used on fuselage sides for PRU Blue painted aircraft. Colors consisted of Dull Blue and Dull Red in a 2:5 ratio. Standard size for Spitfires and Hurricanes was 56in, Mosquitos 54in, Swordfish 56in, and Lancasters 100in.

Type C Roundel. Used on light surfaces from 1942-1947 but excluded from use on upper surfaces from 1942- to early 1945. Colors consisted of Dull Blue, White, and Dull Red in a ratio of 3:4:8. Standard size of 32in for Hurricane and Spitfire from May 1942.

Type C.1 Roundel. Replaced Type A.1 in July 1942. Standard fuselage marking for all RAF/FAA aircraft. Standard size of 36in for Spitfire, Hurricane, Mosquito, and Swordfish, 54in for Lancaster. Appeared on upper wings and fuselages of 2nd TAF bombers from January 1945 to 1947, and on upper, lower and fuselage sides of 2nd TAF fighters during this same period.

Bibliography

Air Publication 2656A, *External Colour of Aircraft*, December 1944
Ministry of Aircraft Production Colour Standards
Air Ministry Orders A.1246/43, A.864/44
British Aviation Colours of World War Two, Volume 3 (Arms and Armour Press, 1976)
Camouflage and Markings: RAF Fighter Command Northern Europe, 1936–45 (Ducimus Books, 1970)

Aircraft Camouflage and Markings, 1907–1954 (Aero Publishers, 1956)
Lancaster in Action (Squadron Signal Publications, 1982)
Hurricane Walkaround (Squadron Signal Publications, 1998)

Index